THE JOURNAL OF A SLAVE TRADER (John Newton)

1750–1754

With Newton's *Thoughts upon the African Slave Trade*

Edited, with an introduction, by

BERNARD MARTIN

and

MARK SPURRELL

LONDON

THE EPWORTH PRESS

FIRST PUBLISHED BY
THE EPWORTH PRESS 1962

Book Steward
FRANK H. CUMBERS

PRINTED AND BOUND IN ENGLAND BY
HAZELL WATSON AND VINEY LTD
AYLESBURY AND SLOUGH

CONTENTS

ILLUSTRATIONS

ACKNOWLEDGEMENTS

THE editors are grateful to the owner of the Journal, Miss Catherine M. Bull, for allowing it to be published. They are indebted, also, to a number of librarians, especially at the Reading Room and Map Departments of The British Museum, The London Library, Dr Williams's Library, The National Maritime Museum, The Public Records Office, The India Office Library, The Colonial Office Library, The Library of the Commonwealth Society, The Admiralty Library and The Royal Geographical Society.

Introduction

JOHN NEWTON (1725–1807)

JOHN NEWTON was born in London in 1725. His mother, a devout woman, taught her only child to read by the time that he was four, and began his arithmetic and Latin lessons before he was six. She died when he was seven.

John's father was master of ships in the Mediterranean trade, a man of unusual qualities, who had been educated in Spain; an honest, upright man, but a stern disciplinarian. Captain Newton married a second time, and John was sent to a boarding-school in Essex where, he said, 'imprudent severity almost broke my spirit and relish for books'.

In his tenth year, John was taken away from school and sent to sea, but his father's 'air of distance and severity' overawed and discouraged the boy. At fifteen he was apprenticed to a Spanish merchant at Alicant, but soon lost his job by 'unsettled behaviour and impatience of restraint'.

By the time that John was seventeen he had passed through various phases of religious experience – an enthusiasm for pious books, fasting, abstinence from eating meat, meditations and prolonged silences, and such 'exceeding wickedness' as blasphemy and cursing. Then he became a Freethinker, learning by heart long passages of Shaftesbury's *Characteristics*, and seeking opportunities to ridicule orthodox Christian belief.

In 1742 a Liverpool merchant, Joseph Manesty, of the firm mentioned in the Journal as J. M. & Co., offered to send him to Jamaica for four or five years to learn the plantation business. Before he was due to leave England, John visited for the first time some friends of his mother, named Catlett, who lived in Chatham. He became so infatuated with Mary Catlett, who was not yet thirteen years of age, that he stayed in Chatham until his ship for Jamaica had sailed. His angry father then sent him as a foremast man in a ship to the Mediterranean – a voyage which lasted about a year. On his return John again visited Mary, and again remained away so long as to upset his father's next plans for him. Then he was caught in the streets of London by a press-gang.

After a month of misery in H.M.S. *Harwich*, young Newton was made a midshipman. War with France began, and H.M.S. *Harwich*, after some convoy work, was in a spirited action with a French man-of-war.

At the end of 1744, H.M.S. *Harwich* was ordered to sail on an East Indies cruise for five years. Newton was given shore leave for one day.

He rode to Chatham to say farewell to Mary Catlett and overstayed his leave. On return to his ship he was reprimanded. H.M.S. *Harwich* sailed from England, but owing to a storm anchored off Plymouth. Newton was put in charge of a boat going into the harbour and instructed to make sure that none of the crew deserted. The temptation was too great. He believed that his father could, somehow, get him transferred from the Royal Navy to The Royal African Company. So he deserted – walking out of Plymouth, afraid to ask which road to take. He walked all day and all night, and part of the next day, and was then arrested by a military patrol, marched back to Plymouth and locked in the town guardhouse. Two days later he was taken aboard his ship and put in irons. Then he was brought before the assembled ship's company, stripped and flogged; after which he was degraded from his office of midshipman and became again a foremast man.

Service in the Royal Navy was used as a threat to maintain discipline in merchantmen, as will be seen in the Journal. Troublesome sailors were put aboard a warship and sometimes a naval commander got rid of unwanted men by 'exchanging' them with a merchantman. When H.M.S. *Harwich* reached Madeira, such an exchange took place with a ship engaged in the slave trade. John Newton pleaded successfully to be one of the two warship men to be exchanged.

Thus he entered the slave trade as foremast man in a ship, which soon sailed from Madeira for Sierra Leone to collect slaves. She was six months slaving and, then, as she was about to sail to the West Indies, the master died. Newton had been troublesome; he had a quick wit and a talent for rhyming, and used to make up songs ridiculing the ship's officers and soon had the whole crew singing them. The mate, when he succeeded to the command, threatened to put Newton aboard a man-of-war when the ship reached the West Indies, 'and this', wrote Newton, 'from what I had known already, was more dreadful to me than death'.

There was a resident slave-dealer in Sierra Leone, a white man named Clow, who was part owner of the ship in which Newton served. Newton got his discharge on condition that he entered Clow's service in Africa. He was very ready to jump at this chance to get free, but he soon found that it was out of the frying-pan into the fire. Clow lived on a small island, one of the Plantanes, with a black 'wife', who is called in the Journal 'P.I.' because her name sounded like those letters. P.I. took a violent dislike to her husband's young white assistant. When Clow was away for a few months searching for slaves, Newton was ill with a fever and P.I. treated him cruelly, denying him water and suitable food and making her black slaves torment him. When Clow returned P.I. prevailed upon him to use Newton as a slave, working with the blacks in a lime-tree plantation, without pay, badly fed, and inadequately clothed. This is the period of Newton's slavery, when he found solace in mastering the first six books of Euclid, drawing the diagrams with a long stick on the wet sand of the sea shore – an experience recounted, almost exactly in Newton's words, in Wordsworth's *Prelude*.[1]

After about a year of this slavery another white dealer came to the Plantanes, and Clow, ashamed to be seen treating a fellow countryman as though he were a negro, released Newton to let him enter the service of the newcomer. Newton was at once reclothed, well fed, and treated as a companion. Soon he was sent with another white man to manage a small factory about a hundred miles away. Meanwhile his father had asked Joseph Manesty of Liverpool to tell his ships' captains to look out for his son and, if possible, bring him home. One day when Newton was short of articles to barter, his companion, seeing a ship on the horizon, made a smoke. The ship, named the *Greyhound*, hove to, and the trader went out to her in a canoe. The captain asked if he had heard of John Newton. At first Newton was reluctant to give up his profitable job and return to England, but at last he was persuaded and went aboard as a kind of supercargo, sharing the captain's cabin, dining at his table and with no service expected of him.

The *Greyhound* was not collecting slaves, but trading for gold, ivory, dyers-wood, and bees-wax. She had been about five months on the Coast and after Newton joined her remained another twelve months trading, sailing another thousand miles down the African coast before starting the homeward passage.

In *An Authentic Narrative*, Newton has described vividly the ordeal of the *Greyhound* in the Atlantic Ocean, storm-driven and becalmed, and during these adventures his conversion from free-thinking to Christianity. When the *Greyhound* got back to Liverpool, Manesty offered Newton the captaincy of one of his ships. Newton was twenty-three years old. He refused, considering himself too inexperienced, but asked to serve as first mate. In that capacity he made one voyage in The *Brownlow*, collecting slaves and transporting them to Charlestown in Carolina where the ship remained for several months. On returning to England, Newton married Mary Catlett and soon after was appointed to his first command, The *Duke of Argyle*, a ship which he later described as 'a very old and crazy vessel . . . hardly fit to lye in a dock or make a Gravesend voyage'. She was 'about 140 tons Burthen'. The Journal describes his voyage in this ship and two subsequent voyages in the *African*.

In 1750, when the Journal begins, the slave trade was not only respectable, but seemed to be indispensable to English prosperity. Slavery was accepted generally without question. There were a few individual protests, of course, and in America some German Quakers had denounced the trade as early as 1688 and other Quakers did so in 1696. In England the first corporate protest came from the Society of Friends in 1727. But Quakers

[1] Book VI, lines 160–74.

were unorthodox and considered to be eccentric – as, to their credit, they were. It was years after Newton left the trade before protests were heard from prominent churchmen such as Bishop Warburton in 1766 and John Wesley in 1774, and thirty-three years before there was enough public support to start a Committee for the Abolition of the Slave Trade.

Newton's attitude to the slave trade during the years that he was engaged in it may be judged from his own comments:
26th January 1753, he wrote: 'The three greatest blessings of which human nature is capable are undoubtedly religion, liberty, and love. In each of these how highly has God distinguished me! ! But here in Africa are whole nations around me, whose languages are entirely different from each other, yet I believe they all agree in this, that they have no words among them expressive of these engaging ideas. . . . These poor creatures are not only strangers to the advantages which I enjoy, but are plunged in all the contrary evils . . . they are deceived and harassed by necromancing, magic, and all the train of superstitions that fear combined with ignorance, can produce in the human mind. The only liberty of which they have any notion, is an exemption from being sold; and even from this very few are perfectly secure . . . for it often happens, that the man who sells another on board a ship, is himself bought and sold, in the same manner, and, perhaps in the same vessel, before the week is ended' (*Letters to a Wife*).
21st March 1753: After almost five years in the trade, including the *Brownlow* voyage, he wrote in his diary, thanking God that he had been led into, 'an easy and creditable way of life'.
21st February 1754: After listing some of his blessings he wrote in his diary of 'the disadvantages of being obliged to pass so much of my time in this distasteful climate and employment'.
June 1756: After recording in his diary how he was obliged to leave the slave trade on account of ill health, he wrote, 'thus I was brought out of a way of life, disagreeable to my temper and inconvenient to my profession [of the Christian faith]'.

By the time he wrote *An Authentic Narrative*, eight years later, he seems to have had doubts about the morality of the trade (see quotation, page 95), and thirty-two years later, in *Thoughts upon the African Slave Trade*, he said: 'I think I should have quitted it [the slave trade] sooner had I considered it as I now do to be unlawful and wrong. But I never had a scruple upon this head at the time; nor was such a thought ever suggested to me by any friend. What I did I did ignorantly; considering it as the line of life which Divine Providence had allotted me. . . .'
Newton's opinion of the Africans he met may be read in *Thoughts upon the African Slave Trade* and in the following answers to direct questions put to him by a committee of the House of Commons in 1790:

'With equal advantages they would be equal to ourselves in point of capacity. I have met with many instances of real and decided natural capacity amongst them.'

'I do not think they are naturally indolent. We hire many of them by the month to work on board our ships and in our boats.'

'The intercourse of the Europeans has assimilated them more to our manners: but I am afraid has rather had a bad than a good influence upon their morals; I mean they learn our customs, they wear our apparel, they get our furniture; but they are generally worse in their conduct in proportion to their acquaintance with us.'

'The most humane and moral people I ever met with in Africa were on the River Gaboon and at Cape Lopas; and they were the people who had the least intercourse with Europe.'

In evidence to the Privy Council in 1789, he said:

'The people [of Sierra Leone] are like European travellers and tell such wonderful stories there is no depending on them.'

'The people [of the Sherbro area] are gentle when they have no communication with the Europeans.'

A year after the Journal ends Newton became a Tide Surveyor in H.M. Customs at Liverpool. During the nine years that he was in this service he came under the influence of Whitefield and Wesley. At the age of thirty-nine he was ordained and appointed curate at Olney. the vicar being an absentee. The poet Cowper, after a year and a half in a lunatic asylum, came to live in Olney and when his madness returned sought refuge in the vicarage where Newton tended him with patience and marked gentleness for thirteen months. Together they wrote the Olney hymns. In 1780 Newton became rector of St Mary Woolnoth in the City of London where his preaching attracted crowds. William Wilberforce came to him for spiritual advice and under Newton's influence Wilberforce threw in his lot with the Abolitionists. In 1788 Newton wrote his effective pamphlet, *Thoughts upon the African Slave Trade,* reprinted in this volume. He gave evidence against the trade to the Privy Council in 1789 and in 1790 to a Committee of the House of Commons. Thus the man who in 1750 began his Journal with a quotation from Virgil. 'It will be pleasant to remember these things hereafter', was haunted in his old age by memories of a 'business at which my heart now shudders'.

The trade in negro slaves was called 'the triangular trade'. One side of the triangle was the voyage from England to the West Coast of Africa with a cargo of varied exports. On arrival the ships sailed up and down the coast selling by barter the goods they had brought, and buying slaves – much of this trading was done in boats which plied between the ship and the many rivers and creeks. This trading often took six to eight months. The second side of the triangle, called the 'middle passage', was between Africa and the West Indies or North America, where the slaves were sold, usually by auction, to plantation owners. The triangle was completed by the homeward passage to England with plantation produce, such as cotton, tobacco, and sugar.

As will be seen from the Journal, navigation was a chancy and anxious business for the master. The latitude could be known reasonably accurately by measuring the height of the sun at noon, but for longitude Newton depended on his reckoning. This was based on the compass for direction and the log, a small board towed astern by which the speed of the ship could be measured, for distance travelled. The log was not an accurate instrument, and also allowance had to be made for drifting to leeward and for currents, so the reckoning was frequently wrong, and when at sea he seldom knew exactly where he was.

In 1790 when Newton gave evidence to a Committee of the House of Commons, he was asked about the effects of the trade on seamen. In his reply he said: 'I suppose there is no trade in which seamen are treated with so little humanity. . . . I have myself seen them when sick beaten for being lazy till they have died under the blows.'

While he was trading he described slave ship crews thus: 'Those who are in the sea service have been generally bred to it young [but] of late years people in creditable life have too much disdained bringing up their children this way. We are for the most part supplied with the refuse and dregs of the nation. The prisons and glass houses furnish us with large quotas and boys impatient of their parents or masters, or already ruined by some untimely vice and for the most part devoid of all good principles. . . .[2]

His own treatment of crews can be judged from the Journal and from the following passage in *Letters to a Wife*, 21st September 1751: 'My condition when abroad and even in Guinea, might be envied by multitudes who stay at home. I am as absolute in my small dominions (life and death excepted) as any potentate in Europe. If I say to one, Come, he comes; if to another, Go, he flies. If I order one person to do something, perhaps three or four will be ambitious of a share in the service. Not a man in the ship must eat his dinner till I please to give him leave; nay, nobody dares to say it is twelve or eight o'clock in my hearing, till I think proper to say so first. There is a mighty bustle of attendance when I leave the ship and a strict watch kept while I am absent, lest I should return unawares, and not be received in due form. And should I stay out till midnight (which for that reason I never do without necessity) nobody must presume to shut their eyes till they have had the honour of seeing me again. I would have you judge from my manner of relating these ceremonials, that I do not value them highly for their own sake; but they are old-established customs

[2] Unpublished letter to Dr David Jennings, 29th August 1752 (Dr Williams's Library; Ref. 38.98.50).

and necessary to be kept up; for, without a strict discipline, the common sailors would be unmanageable. But in the midst of all my parade, I do not forget (I hope I never shall) what my situation was on board the *Harwich* and at the Plantanes [in the service of Clow].'

In 1788, thirty-four years after the Journal ends, Newton wrote, as anti-slavery propaganda, *Thoughts upon the African Slave Trade*. He told William Cowper that it was written 'without solicitation', and Cowper described it as 'the most satisfactory publication on the subject'. It is here printed as an appendix (pages 98–113) because it gives such an admirable account of the general conditions of trading.

It is believed that Newton's Journal is unique as a complete day-to-day record of the negro slave trade at the middle of the eighteenth century, from the point of view of a slave ship's captain, but the reader is referred to a record entitled *Journal of a Slave-Dealer* (Routledge, 1930) with the sub-title, *A view of some remarkable Axcedents in the life of Nics Owen on the Coast of Africa and America from the Year 1746 to the Year 1757*. Part of this interesting record related to sea voyages to America and the West Indies, but Owen lived in Sierra Leone for several years as a resident slave-dealer from about the time when Newton's Journal ends. His record gives a good impression of the life of the few white men who resided in Africa at that time. He mentions a few of the dealers and captains named by Newton.

From the point of view of the slave, there is an autobiography of one who was carried off from West Africa as a boy of under twelve, a year or two after Newton was trading on the coast. He was kidnapped far inland and, after changing hands several times, was eventually sold to a slave ship and taken to the West Indies. He obtained his freedom, and in 1789 wrote his autobiography, entitled *The interesting narrative of the life of Olaudah Equiano, or Gustavus Vassa, the African, written by himself*.

It may be useful to add a note here on the currency use in the trade. The denominator used in barter was called in Sierra Leone a 'bar' – elsewhere on the West African coast it was called a 'piece', an 'ackey', a 'pawn', and a 'copper'.[3]
Originally a bar was a piece of iron brought from England; in 1710 these bars cost three shillings and sixpence each in London, and when delivered in Africa, five shillings.[4] As other goods were introduced – ironmongery, textiles, guns, gunpowder, beer, cider, and spirits – they were valued in bars, for example a gun might be ten bars, a length of cloth eight bars, a gallon of brandy three bars. A slave was bought at a certain number of bars, agreed after haggling between seller and buyer. The seller then selected articles from the varied assortment of goods offered by the buyer,

[3] See *A Voyage to the River Sierra Leone*, John Matthews (London, 1791).

[4] *A True State of the present differences between the Royal African Company and the Seperate Traders* (London, 1710).

to the agreed number of bars. The value of a bar varied from time to time and place to place and there was sometimes a difference between 'country bars' and 'ship's bars'. Moreover, bars were sometimes divided into shillings and pence – thus Owen values one kettle at four country bars, or, in ship's bars, two bars two shillings and six pence. Still more confusing is the fact that in the same account Owen has two real iron bars which are valued at two country bars or 2 ship's bars. The whole assortment of goods in this account is valued at twenty country bars or, in ship's bars, thirty-six bars one shilling and sixpence. In comparison with this Irishman's accounts Newton's are quite simple – he mentions only one kind of bar and does not go into details.

THE MANUSCRIPT AND METHOD OF EDITING

Burney's Maritime Dictionary describes the main purpose of a journal as being to record what winds and currents a ship meets with so that, with the observation and log, the ship's position could be fixed. A journal should also include an account of all ships and lands sighted, and of the general condition of the crew and ship. Newton's Journal conforms to Burney's definition, but is more than an ordinary ship's journal in that a large part of it is concerned with trading. In ships of the East India Company the master, the first mate and the second mate were all required to keep a journal which had to be handed over to the company at the end of the voyage,[5] but the practice in slave ships probably varied. As Newton's Journal records three voyages in one volume it is probable that it was not intended to be handed over to the owners. When he gave evidence to the Privy Council in 1789 he mentioned that he had this Journal before him and also another journal (which cannot now be traced) which he kept when he was first mate in the *Brownlow*.

The Journal fills 336 pages of a leather-bound foolscap book. Entries were made almost daily over a period of four years, at sea, in ships of about 150 tons, sometimes in storms, usually in a humid atmosphere, so that it is remarkable that the manuscript is still in good condition. As can be seen from the facsimile at page 37 the handwriting is clear and uniform. Quite short words are split sometimes to fill a line. In editing, the original spelling has mostly been retained. Abbreviations have usually been expanded: 'ye' is printed 'the', and the past tense written 'd' is changed to 'ed'. The punctuation and frequent use of initial capitals have been amended, and the dating of entries has been standardized.

While at sea Newton's entries ran from noon to noon, but when the ship was trading on the coast or at anchor, he reverted to the land usage, midnight to midnight. At sea '*Tuesday 25th September*' for example, covers the period from noon Monday 24th to noon Tuesday 25th.

The first voyage (131 pages of MS) is here printed in full except that

[5] In 1860 these East India Co. journals were destroyed.

navigational details and daily weather reports are usually omitted, the omissions being indicated by dots. All references to other ships are included. The second voyage (113 pages of MS) and the third voyage (92 pages of MS) are much abbreviated, including only entries which differ in kind or degree from the first voyage.

Editorial comment where the sense is doubtful, and quotations from complementary documents are enclosed within square brackets. There is a short glossary on page 114.

COMPLEMENTARY DOCUMENTS

Newton's Diaries (unpublished). For the period covered by the Journal there is a diary from 22nd December 1751 to 5th July 1754, mainly concerned with his spiritual life.

Letters to Mary Newton. Newton wrote frequent letters to his wife while he was at sea. Some were published in 1793 after her death, entitled *Letters to a Wife,* and there are a few others which have survived but have not been published.

Letters to the Rev. David Jennings, D.D. (unpublished). Now in Dr Williams's Library and here quoted by permission of the Trustees and Librarian. Dr David Jennings was Congregational minister in Stepney, at the church where Newton's mother was a member. See also *Dictionary of National Biography.*

An Authentic Narrative. An autobiogaphy to the year 1763, published 1764 and many times reprinted in America and in England.

Thoughts upon the African Slave Trade. Published 1788. This pamphlet is not included in Newton's collected works in most of the English or American editions. It is here included in full as an appendix because it is the best general account of slave trading at the middle of the century and because it gives Newton's considered and final opinion of the trade.

Newton's evidence to the Privy Council, 1789. British Museum, 524.K.14.

Newton's evidence to a Committee of the House of Commons, 11th and 12th May 1790. State Papers, British Museum, Vol. LXXXVIII, pp. 137 ff.

BIBLIOGRAPHICAL NOTE

Newton is the subject of two biographies:

John Newton, by Josiah Bull, M.A. (London, 1868).

John Newton, by Bernard Martin (Heinemann, 1950; revised and retitled, *An Ancient Mariner*, Wyvern Books, 1960).

There are many references to Newton in books about English Literature, the Slave Trade, West Africa, and Hymns. The most important are to be found in works relating to William Cowper, William Wilberforce, Hannah More, and Wordsworth.

The First Voyage

11TH AUGUST 1750—17TH OCTOBER 1751

Journal

Kept on board the Duke of Argyle, Snow [1]

from Liverpool to Africa,

Commenced the 11th August

1750

Qui mare fluctisonum sulcat, curvisque carinis
Admovet externas vaga per commercia gentes,
Non ignota illi divina potentia, nec quae
Monstrat in immenso miracula saepe profundo.

BUCHANAN IN PSALM 107 [2]

Olim haec meminisse juvabit. [3]

[1] A ship like a brig, see illustration on page 117.

[2] An eighteenth-century paraphrase of Psalm 107:23–4 reads:

Such as in Ships and brittle Barks into the Seas descend
Their Merchanidize thro' fearful Floods to compass and to end:
These men are forcèd to behold the Lord's Works what they be;
And in the dreadful Deep the same most marvellous they see.

[3] It will be pleasant to remember these things hereafter—After VIRGIL.

Sailors belonging to the *Duke of Argyle*. 1750

Names	*Quality*
John Newton	Master
John Bridson	1st Mate, deceased 20th January
Samuel Marshall	2nd do.
John Hamilton	3rd do.
Robert Arthur	Surgeon, deceased 17th August
Andrew Corrigall	Carpenter, deceased 11th January
John Hallin	Boatswain
John Carren	Cooper
James Johnson	Gunner, discharged 18th July
Joseph Fellows	Steward
Mark Couture	Cook
Matthew Curfey	Taylor
Thomas Creed	Fore the mast – put on board the *Surprize*, 25th November
William Barber	do. Discharged 15th July
Thomas True	do. Put on board the *Surprize*, 25th November
John Corkhill	do.
Thomas Brown	do. Discharged 15th July
Owen Cavana	do. Put on board the *Surprize*, 25th November
William Lees	do. Put on board the *Surprize*, 22nd November
James Pitts	do. Discharged 7th August
Edward Cathorn	do. Discharged 3rd August
David Thompson	do. Discharged 7th August
John Thomas	do.
Thomas Peirce	Ordinary
Edward Lawson	do. Deceased 18th December
Gideon Meacham	do. Deceased 7th June
James Gallagher	Fidler do.
Thomas Bridson	Ship's Apprentice, deceased 29th March 1751
James Morgan	do.
Robert Cropper	do.

Entered from on board the *Surprize*, 25th November

William Lapworth	Discharged 3rd August
William Puckett	Deceased 7th January
John Seringer	
John Hymus	

Laus Deo

Journal of a voyage intended (by God's permission) in the Duke of Argyle, *snow, John Newton, Master, from Liverpool to the Windward Coast of Africa, etc; commenced the 11th August 1750.*

Saturday 11th August. Close weather, fresh gales between the South and West. At noon cast from the pier head at Liverpool, run under the topsails against the flood, at 3 p.m. anchored at Black Rock with the B.B. Upon the ebb, mored with the sheet anchor, hoisted in the longboat and punt. Came down and anchored with us the *Lamb,* Job Lewis,[1] for New England. In the evening small rain.

Sunday 12th August. Mostly fair weather, fresh gales about SW. Arrived the *Beverley,* brig, from Barbadoes and a snow from the Isle of Man.

Monday 13th August. Fair weather, variable winds between the South and West. In the morning rigged the spreetsail yard and jib boom: bent the mainsail, sprit sail jib and staysails. Backed out the starboard backstay plate bolt forward; the link being broke, sent it to town [Liverpool]. In the afternoon a pilot boat brought our powder on board. Arrived the *Golden Lyon,* Patterson, from Greenland, and a snow from St Kitts. Came down 2 small brigs, and a ship for Dublin, and a Dane.

[1] Throughout the Journal Newton puts the captain's name, when known, after the name of the ship.

Tuesday 14th August. All day fair weather and little winds, variable. At 8 a.m. came on to blow strong from the SSE. with rain: lowered the low yards. Towards midnight cleared up a little and wind backed to the SSW. and blew very hard. Fixed the new trysail.

Wednesday 15th August. The first part cloudy weather and very hard gales at WSW., the latter fair and moderate. People at work making sinnet, swabs, etc.; fixed the boats gripes and stoppers for the cables. In the evening 3 of our people, Owen Cavana, Thomas True and Thomas Peirse left the boat on shoar and went up to town. Fixed the yaul's sails.

Thursday 16th August. Squally weather, wind about SW. In the morning swayed up the lower yards. People at work making sinnet, etc. Carpenter mended the channel bend, and fixed the backstay plate. Shipped Mr Samuel Marshall, second mate, in the room of Mr Whipp and sent the latter's chest on shoar. Pilot boat came on board with fresh provisions.

> [From a letter of this date to Dr Jennings: 'I am now nearly ready for the sea and believe I shall sail with the first Easterly wind if settled weather. A Guinea voyage is a great charge, and more particularly difficult at this time: had I no farther dependance, than on my own diligence foresight and prudence . . . I should hardly expect a tolerable success and satisfaction; tho I think I shall spare no pains and understand the business perhaps as well as my Neighbours: But on the other hand when I consider, that in the most inhospitable climate and the most distressed circumstances I shall be surrounded with a Providence always able, always ready, to supply my every deficiency and to further all my designs, if really conducive to my true interest . . . I then grow composed and ready to undertake whatever is necessary with chearfulness. . . . Having been detained a fortnight by contrary winds and the time you appointed for being here, elapsed, I hope to have the pleasure of paying you my respects *viva voce*.']

Fryday 17th August. Cloudy weather, fresh gales about SW. People employed as yesterday. Fixed the longboat's sails.

Saturday 18th August. Till towards evening fair weather, fresh breases about SSE., afterwards squally with rain, wind variable from SSW. to WSW. At 10 a.m. the pilot came on board, brought a sheep and a quarter of beef. Began to unmoor in order to sail, but when we had took up our ebb anchor in the boat the *Lamb's* anchor was foul of our sheet cable. The ebb being made, and we [not] able to shoot clear, were obliged to let go again, or should have been on board. Were employed till 2 p.m. in clearing our cable, and then being too late with the tide to proceed, were obliged to moor again with half a cable each way, as did the *Lamb*, but most of the other outward bound got out.

Sunday 19th August. Fair weather, the first part strong gales westerly, the latter moderate. In the morning a brig and 2 sloops that sailed yesterday came in and run up to town; informed us that most of the others are put into Hyle Lake [Hoylake].

Monday 20th August. Till noon.[2] Very fair weather, variable winds and calms. At 10 a.m., having a small air about N, unmored, and, hove a peak upon our ebb anchor, sent the yaul with 4 hands to assist Captain Lewis. At ½ past 11, eleven being the top of high water, weighed in company with the *Lamb*: at noon are working with a small brease at North.

[From this date until 18th October, while the ship is outward bound, a log table is included every day. See illustration, page 6.]

Tuesday 21st August. The first part fair weather and calm, the latter very thick and fresh gales. Towed down Fromby Channel with the yaul and punt, and at 6 p.m., being low water, anchored a league without the NW. buoy as did the *Lamb* and a Dane, and likewise weighed with us at midnight. Went under foresail, topsails, trysail and forestaysail till 3 a.m., then sat mainsail, and took 1 reaf in the fore and 2 in the main topsail: at 6 let 1 out and sat the jibb and main topmast staysail. At 8 the land of Ormshead bore as per log; at 10 sat middle stay sail, at noon got down top gallant yards and tacked to the southward. Ramsay Head bearing as per log [Log entry is 'NNW. 7 legs']. The *Lamb* and Dane stood on for the Island [Isle of Man]. Got the B.B. anchor in upon the forecastle, and the sheet anchor upon the gunnel.

Wednesday 22nd August. Fair weather, light gales as per log, and calms. At 6 p.m. anchored (the Calf of Man bearing NW. b N. 8 leag, the welsh land near Beaumaris SW. 10 leagues) at two graplins lashed and bent to the towline. At midnight weighed, stood to the northward till 2 a.m., then tacked, at 5½ tacked again and at 7 came too with the graplins in 26 fathoms, the same Welsh land bearing SSW., and a point without which, suppose near Holy head, SW. b W.; the Calf of Man bearing NNW. Veered out the whole towline, but dragged a little the whole flood. Almost calm. Fitted the new jibb.

Thursday 23rd August. At 1 p.m. weighed with light gales as per log, and fine weather. Found 2 flukes of one grablin gone, and one of the other broke. Stood in till 5 then tacked off. At 7 came too with the sheet anchor in 28 fathoms, Holy head bearing SW. and the Calf of Man NNW. At midnight, being slack water, weighed, stood to the northward, at 2 tacked, at 4 tacked to the northward again, at 7 let out the reafs and sat

[2] The entry is for the morning only.

small staysail, at 10 came on to blow very fresh, handed jib and staysails and [took] 2 reafs in each topsail, at 11 tacked to the southward to keep in the southern tide, the Calf of Man bearing N. b E. and Holyhead SSW. See 2 sail standing to the northward. Mem: the tide sets E ½ S and W ½ N where we came too last night, and not less than 3½ miles per hour.

Fryday 24th August. Thick weather with rain in the night, strong and at times very hard gales as per log. At 4 p.m. wore and stood off, Holy head bearing SSW. 6 leagues. Handed the trysail and foretopsail, and soon after maintopsail; lashed and frapped the boats to the scuppers. At midnight wore in, handed foresail, tryed under a mainsail till 4 a.m., blowing exceeding hard, and a high irregular sea, then wore and sat foresail. At 6 the Calf of Man bore N b E. 6 leagues; having a whole flood coming against us, and not able to clear the land upon either tack, and looking very dirty to the westward, bore away for Ramsay Bay; sat single reafed topsails, at 10 were abreast of Douglass, took in the other reaf in the topsails, and unstowed the anchors. At noon are almost up with Ramsay Head, a snow and brigg standing in before us, blows exceeding hard in squalls.

Saturday 25th August. At ½ past noon were open of Ramsay Bay, halled close in. Blew so very hard at times that could scarce suffer a fore sail and maintopsail and trysail, with which we made four trips under the land and gained ground, tho the ebb was made. At 1½ p.m. came too with the sheet anchor in 8 fathoms off the south end of the town. In the road his Majesty's ship the *Amazon*, 2 Dutch and 2 English vessels, besides the 2 that came in with us. Continues very bad weather.

All night had a very wild sky, the Aurorae Borealis or Northern Lights flying about with unusual quickness. After daylight came on extream thick, and the gale encreased. At noon blows a meer frett; clinched the cables round the main mast, and veered the sheet cable to the better end. Struck the top-gallant masts.

Sunday 26th August. Mostly very thick weather and excessive hard gales about WSW. and West. At 2 p.m. let go the starboard anchor under foot. Arrived a snow from the northward and a Dutchman from the southward.

Monday 27th August. Variable weather and winds, sometimes blowing extream hard, sometimes moderate. At 2 p.m. took up the starboard anchor, and at 4 shortned in the other, but was obliged to veer away at 9. Two coasting briggs sailed in the afternoon but put back in the night. At 8 a.m. the *Amazon* sailed for Douglas. At 10 looking like fair weather. swayed up the top-gallant masts and lower yards, and at noon are just under way with an easy brease at WNW.

Tuesday 28th August. Very unsettled winds and weather. Before had got 2 miles round the head fell calm, and at 3 p.m. came on a fresh gale at SW.

... the Duke of Argyle from Liverpool for Africa ... 1750.

H	K	HF	Courses	Winds
2	-	-	SSE	SW
4	-	-	----	Wore
6	-	-	WNW	S
8	-			......
10	-	-	WbN	SWbS
12	-		......	Wore
2	Up	SEbS off SbE		
4	-	-	....	Wore
6	-	-	NbW	WbN
8	Bore away for			Ramsay
10	-		- - -	WSW
12	-		......	......

Fryday ye 24th August

Thick weather, with rain in the night, strong & at times very hard Gales as p Log, at 4 PM wore & stood off Holy head bearing SSW 6 Leagues, handed the trysail & foretopsail, & soon after Maintopsail, lashd & frapp'd the Boats to the Scuppers at midnight wore in, handed foresail, tryd under a mainsail till 4 AM, blowing exceeding hard, & a high irregular sea, then wore & sat Foresail, at 6 the Calf of man bore NbE 6 Leagues, having a whole flood coming against us, & not able to clear the Land upon either tack, & looking very dirty to ye Westward, bore away for Ramsay Bay, set single reefd topsails at 10 were abreast of Douglass, took the other reef in ye topsails, & unstowd the anchors, at noon are almost up with Ramsay head a Snow & Brig, standing in before us, blows exceeding hard in squalls.

H	K	HF	Courses	Winds
2	Anchord in 8 fathoms			W...
4	-		- - - -	....
6	-		- - - -	....
8	-		- - - -	....
10	-		- - -	WNW
12	-		.....	.....
2	-		.....	....
4				
6				
8				
10	-		.....	.....
12	-		.....	.....

Saturday ye 25th August

At ½ past noon were open of Ramsay bay, hauld close in blew so very hard at times, that could scarce suffer a fore sail & maintopsail & trysail, with which we made 4 trips under the Land, & gaind ground, tho the Ebb was made at 1½ PM came too with the Sheet Anchor in 8 fathoms off the So end of ye town. In the road his Majestys Ship the Amazon, 2 Dutch & 2 English Vessels besides the 2 that came in with us, continues very bad weather.

All night had a very wild sky, the Aurora Boreales or Northern Lights flying about with unusual quickness, after daylight came on extream thick, & the gale encreasd. at Noon blows a meer fret, clinchd the Cable round the Main mast & veerd the Best Cable to the better end. Struck the Top-gallant masts.

and looked likely to blow. Bore away again, at 4 calm, hoisted out the punt and towed into the road, at 5 anchored without all the ships in 7 fathoms. The first part of the night had the wind at South and SSE.; very squally and dark; about 3 a.m. settled at SW. and blew very hard till 7, then moderated and backed more to the west-ward. Arrived a brig from the northwards.

Wednesday 29th August. The former part variable winds and weather, the latter settled fair as per log. At 2 a.m. weighed, at 5 got up T. gallant yards, sat the sails and turned out all reafs, sat spritsail and at 8 steering sails fore and aft. 4 sail came out with us and are all in sight. At noon the Calf of Man bears NE. 7 leagues, Holy head SE. b S. 9 leagues.

Thursday 30th August. Hazey weather, fresh gales variable. At 6 p.m. halled down steering sails, firled top gallant sails and took a reaf in each topsail. At 5 a.m. wind flew to the SW. and came on extream thick. At 6 had a glimpse of the land, but could not know it, sounded and found 18 fathoms, tacked and stood of till 11, when had 34 fathoms, tacked in, took the other reaf in each top sail. Sound every half hour. Have passed 3 sail near, all plyers. At noon 28 fathoms fine sand.

Friday 31st August. Till day light extream thick weather, afterwards fair. At 1 p.m., having 25 fathoms, tacked. At 2 passed and spoke the *Elizabeth*, Hayes, from Liverpool for Jamaica. At 2 had 33 fathoms, and at 4, 45, the ground coarser as water deepened. At 8 tacked in, and at 9 handed the fore and at 10 the M.T.S., at 11 tacked having 40 fathoms. At 3 a.m. wore to the westward, split the trysail, at 6 sat topsails, unbent the trysail and bent the new one. Saw the land of Dublin to the NW. and W.; at 10 a.m. tacked to the southward. The sugar loaf hill bearing WNW., we being about 5 leagues from the land; 7 sail plyers in sight, 2 passed bound in. In the evening got down top-gallant yards.

Saturday 1st September. Hazey weather, the first part little winds and calms, the latter fresh gales as per log with a following sea. At 2 a.m. let the reaf out the M.T. sail, at 4 got up top-gallant yards and sat the sails, and 2 topmast steering sails abaft, and at 8 the lower topmast steering sails forward. At 9 a.m. the land of St Davidshead bore SEE. ½ E, distance 9 leagues, and at noon the high land about Waterford, NNW. At 8 a.m. counted ten sail, but at noon are all seperated.

Sunday 2nd September. Hazey weather, fresh gales as per log. At 6 p.m. the high land of Dungarvan bore N. b W. 9 leagues. At Sunsett observed the amplitude by a brass-box compass with sights and found the variation as under. Halled down the steering sails. At 11 a.m. took in T.G. sails and took a reaf in the M.T.S. Have seen 2 sail standing to the Eastward. Indifferent smooth water. I reckon Cape Clear bears at noon North 8 leagues, from whence take my departure.

[Newton here enters the start for his dead reckoning.]

Magnetical Amplitude	W°	25·30 N°
True Amplitude	W°	6·30
Variation		19° in Western
Lattitude per Account.		50° 48^{m}

Monday 3rd September. . . . At noon some small rain, had an indifferent observation. . . .

[From this date until a landfall was made at Sierra Leone there are daily entries, but when they are only weather or navigational details they are here omitted.]

* * *

Thursday 13th September. . . . Begin to be sensible of a change of climate. . . . At 9 a.m. saw a large ship to the southward, halled up SW. to get to windward, being apprehensive of the Barbary cruizers; at 11 passed her about 2 miles distance. She hoisted first a french Jack at the mizen-peak, but when we shewed our ensign, they hoisted a French ensign at the staff. . . .

* * *

Wednesday 19th September. Hazey weather with some small rain in the night, a small northern swell. . . . Observed the amplitude at sunsett. . . . Am surprized to find so much variation, for it is but customary to allow but half a point in this latitude and longitude: should suspect by that that I am to the eastward of the island, but that I think it next to impossible to be so much mistaken in our short run, and with the continual fine weather we have had.

* * *

Friday 21st September. . . . At 4 p.m. made the land right ahead, proved the island Grand Canaries; soon after saw the peak of Tenariff, W. ½ S., a great distance, reckoned about 25 leagues. . . . By a good observation I find that my octant agrees very well with the latitude laid down in the tables in the *Mariners' Compass.* If the longitude in the charts and tables are anything near the truth, we must have come between Madera and Port Sancto, tho think it strange that we saw neither. I am consequently not less than 50 leagues to the eastward of my reckoning, which as we have had constant fair winds and weather and frequent observations, must be owing to a strong current setting to the eastward, which cannot suppose

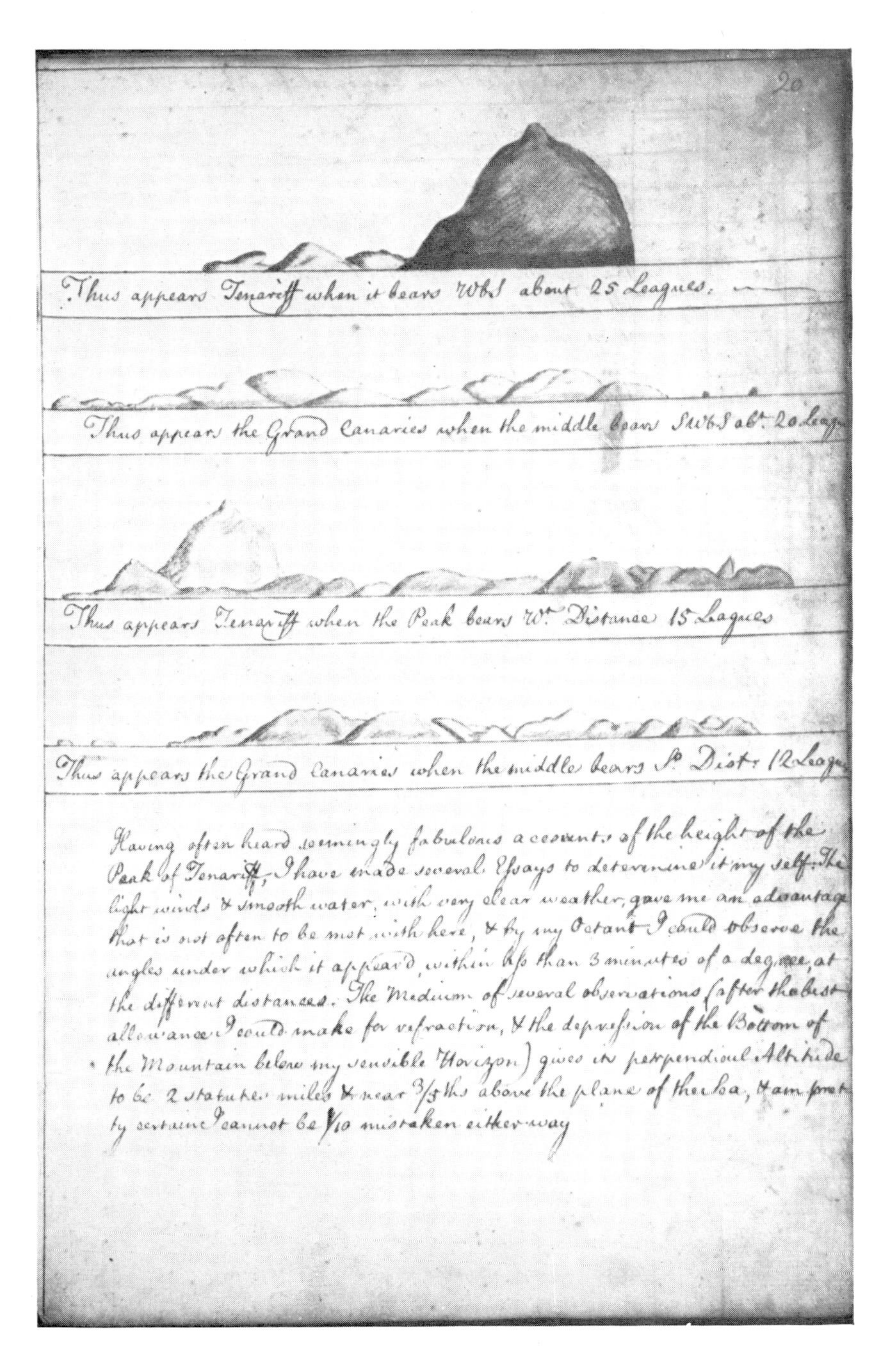

20

Thus appears Tenariff when it bears WbS about 25 Leagues.

Thus appears the Grand Canaries when the middle bears SWbS abt. 20 Leag[ues]

Thus appears Tenariff when the Peak bears Wt. Distance 15 Leagues

Thus appears the Grand Canaries when the middle bears So. Dist: 12 Leag[ues]

Having often heard seemingly fabulous accounts of the height of the Peak of Tenariff, I have made several Essays to determine it my self. The light winds & smooth water, with very clear weather, gave me an advantag[e] that is not often to be met with here, & by my Octant I could observe the angles under which it appear'd, within less than 3 minutes of a degree, at the different distances. The Medium of several observations (after the best allowance I could make for refraction, & the depression of the Bottom of the Mountain below my sensible Horizon) gives its perpendicul Altitude to be 2 statute miles & near 3/5ths above the plane of the Sea, & am pret-ty certain I cannot be 1/10 mistaken either way

Sketch of Canary Islands in Journal

less than 20 miles *per diem* from the time we passed the parallel of Cape St Vincent or 37°.

* * *

Tuesday 25th September. . . . In the afternoon opened Gomera [One of the Canary Islands] out to the westward of Tenariff . . . but the horizon was too hazey to draw it with any exactness. At 6 a.m. hoisted out the punt to try the current, found it set due SW. about ¾ of a mile per hour, but I believe it ran much stronger in the afternoon. People at work upon the cables. Carpenter begun to raise the gratings of the women's room. . . .[3]

Wednesday 26th September. Till 4 p.m. calm, afterwards a small air . . . hazey weather, and water as smooth as oyl. . . . Made an end of serving the cables and boats' ropes. Unbent the M.T.G. sail for a quater deck awning and bent the new. Have taken a new departure from Tenariff.

* * *

Saturday 29th September. . . . This morning reeved a rope at the main-yard arm in complyance with the customary form observed in crossing the tropicks. Had 8 new men who all consented to pay. . . .[4]

* * *

Monday 1st October. . . . A great many flying fish about us; at 8 a.m. passed a large turtle. . . .

Tuesday 2nd October. . . . At 6 a.m. perceived the water to change, and at 7 brought to and sounded but could get no ground with 60 fathoms of line; did not think it worth while to lose time by trying again, but beleive we are upon the bank that lies about mid channel between Cape de Verde and the islands, but by our observations it lies farther to the northwards than it is placed in the charts. . . .

Wednesday 3rd October. . . . At 2 p.m. the water began to change to a deep sea colour again, we running off the West side of the bank. If it

[3] Newton always refers to slaves as 'men' and 'women' and to his crews as 'people'.

[4] The ceremony of crossing the line was observed at the tropic of Cancer, not at the equator. The 'new men' consented to pay for drinks all round to escape the ducking.

'On these occasions, all the people on board a ship who have not passed it before, are subject to a fine, which, if they refuse to pay, or cannot procure, they must be ducked; that is hoisted up by a rope to the yard arm, and from thence dropped souse into the water. This is such fine sport to the seamen, that they would rather lose some of the forfeiture (which is usually paid in brandy) than that every body should escape the ducking. And in many vessels, they single out some poor helpless boy or landsman, to be half drowned for the diversion of his shipmates. But as I do not choose to permit any arbitrary or oppressive laws to be valid in my peaceful kingdom, I always pay for those who cannot pay for themselves.'—From a letter to Mary Newton; 27th July 1752, during the second voyage.

really lies North and South as placed in the chart, it would not be more than 2 miles broad where we run over, but suppose it to lye nearer NW. and SE. I find by my observations that it extends at least 10 leagues farther to the northward than the books reckon it.

Thursday 4th October. . . . Payed the awning the second time with rezin and oyl, then covered it with old canvas. . . .

Carpenter employed in fitting up the stateroom to serve as a shop on the Coast.

Fryday 5th October. . . . The stateroom being finished, begun a rummidge in the hold, removed most of the India cloth and a sortment of other goods into the cabbin, drew off a pipe of spirits into cags, and got the ship's arms chest aft. Were all hands so engaged that lost our observation. Had a ripling of a current the first part of the night.

Saturday 6th October. . . . Made an end of our overhall in the hold; got room to strike down 5 buts of bread, most of the lumber and the small bower cable from betwixt decks, that the carpenter may be able to begin upon the bulk heads on Monday, *Deo adjuvante*. . . .

* * *

Monday 8th October. . . . Made a thorough rummage between decks, halled up both bowers and quoiled them down again in a shorter teer; marked off the slaves' rooms, and the carpenter began to build the bulkheads. Gunner making cartridges, etc., for the carriage and swivel guns. . . .

The water still continues of a deep sea colour, that am in hopes I am not mistaken much in my reckoning, according to which I should be 60 leagues to the westward of the shoals, but am cautious, having had frequent experience of a strong indraught hereabouts.

* * *

Wednesday 10th October. . . . The carpenter having this morning finished the fore bulkhead, hoisted out the punt and hung her over the larboard gunwale, that he may begin to prepare the yaul's deck, powder room, etc. Cleaned and loaded the small arms. Scraped the decks fore and aft. Caught a small dolphin. All sails sat.

* * *

Fryday 12th October. . . . Frequent squalls of rain with a great deal of lightning and thunder. Very strong riplings, at times roaring all round us, almost as loud as London Bridge. A jumbling swell several ways. . . .

Saturday 13th October. . . . At noon lowered down the punt to try the current, by which means unexpectedly found soundings which I had no thoughts of in this latitude; am therefore confirmed in my beleif that the ship is much farther to the eastward than my reckoning; have about 30 fathoms water, coarse red sand with small broken shells. The current sets SE. more than a mile per hour, but suspect it to be the regular tide which ebbs and flows along shoar. A great many sunfish and sharks about us; caught one of the latter.

* * *

Tuesday 16th October. . . . At 2 p.m. got soundings again about 30 fathoms, white sand and black stones. Sounded every 2 hours after and had much the same depth, till the 2 last casts, when had 45 fathoms, the ground very changeable but mostly rocky. . . . Hoisted out the punt and scrubbed the bends, having grass growing above a foot long.

Wednesday 17th October. Very variable winds and weather, sometimes all sails sat with a pretty brease, at others all handed in expectation of a tornado, having a great deal of lightning and thunder. . . .

Thursday 18th October. . . . Cut the longboat's and yaul's sails, for find that they will not stand with gaffs, the topmasts being too weak. This day the carpenter finished his work upon the yaul, and I am in hopes she will be as compleat and commodious as any boat of her size upon the Coast.

Fryday 19th October. . . . Saw the land, Sierra Leon, bearing SE. 16 leagues, and the largest island of the Idolo's NE. b E. 7 leagues. . . . I find that I was too hasty in condemning my reckoning, for it has answered to a great exactness, but cannot place it to my own merit, for the currents we have met with this fortnight past have been too various and confused to be well accounted for, unless by chance. But am pretty certain there are soundings farther to the westward of the shoals of Grande than is generally thought.

['The passage from England has not been the shortest, but remarkably pleasant, and free from disaster.

Last night we were disturbed by a tornado, which I believe I have told you is a violent squall of wind, accompanied with heavy rain, thunder, and lightning. The darkness of the night added to the horror of the scene. But with proper care, under the blessing of Providence these boisterous visitants, though very troublesome, are seldom dangerous; nor do they often last above an hour.'—From *Letters to a Wife*.]

Saturday 20th October. . . . At noon the high land over Cape Sierra Leon, SE. ½ S. 11 leagues; have 14 fathoms water, red sand. All sails sat. Can just see the Banana's from the deck. [The Bonanoe Island.]

* * *

Monday 22nd October. Hazey weather. At 1 p.m. fell calm and continued till 8, then had a small brease at SW. till midnight, afterwards fell calm again. At daylight a small air sprung up about South, at which time the high land of Sierra Leon East 7 leagues, having had a current setting us off all night. . . .

Tuesday 23rd October. Fair weather, land and sea brease. In the afternoon, steering for the Bonanoes. Fell in with the *Cornwall*, Duncan. I went on board him in the punt, and he told me that the white men are all gone from the Bonanoes, upon which I bore away with him for Sierra Leon. He informed me that he had been 6 months on the coast, and that he came on at this place, and had been down at Annamaboe [Anomabu, in Ghana], yet had purchased but about 50 slaves. At 10 p.m. we came both to an anchor in 11 fathoms. . . . At daylight weighed again being near half flood, hoisted out the yaul and towed athwart the tide, having very little wind. . . . At 2 p.m. having a sea brease sufficient to overhall the ebb, weighed, and at sunsett anchored in Frenchman's Bay in 15 fathoms. In the harbour the *Annapolis,* Cleavland, of London, almost slaved; the *Hallifax*, Ellis, of Bristol; a New England schooner and sloop; and three small french-men: the *Williamsburg*, Taite, of Bristol, sailed this morning downwards [southwards – down the coast].

Wednesday 24th October. Fair weather, land and sea brease. At daylight hoisted out the long-boat and the Carpenter began to work upon her, lashed the booms up to the masts and cleared the decks, got the guns up and run them out, and fixed an awning upon the maindeck. In the afternoon mored with the sheet-anchor; made one trip with the yaul for water. In the evening upon my return from on board Captain Ellis [the *Hallifax*], the offisers and all the ship's company to a man complained that the Boatswain had behaved very turbulently, and used them ill, to the hindrance of the ship's business. Having passed by several of the like offences before, I thought it most proper to put him in irons, *in terrorem*, being apprehensive he might occasion disturbance, when we get slaves on board.

Thursday 25th October. Fair weather, easy land and sea brease. In the morning I went down on board Mr Langton's shallop in the White man's bay to view some slaves; was shewn 7, out [of] which I picked 3, viz: 2 men and 1 woman, brought them up and payed the goods for them. In the afternoon ran up with the flood and sea brease to the factory at George's Island.[5] Got there about 10, found the Cheif was indisposed and gone to bed. The yaul employed watering. The carpenter at work upon the longboat.

[5] Known also as Bence, Bance, Bunce, and Benee Island. The Royal African Company built a factory there which was destroyed in 1728 by rival traders led by an Afro-Portuguese. It was later taken over by various independent London merchants. In 1752 their claim to it was confirmed by Act of Parliament.

Fryday 26th October. Wind and weather as yesterday. In the morning had an interview with the Cheif, Mr Staples. He received me with all due civility, but told me in very plain terms, that he was determined to have as little dealings as possible with any body belonging to the town of Liverpool. Staid dinner with him, and then rowed down with the ebb, got on board about 8 p.m., find that the yaul has filled all the buts in the hold.

Saturday 27th October. Fair weather, easy land and sea brease. Put a cargoe in the yaul and sent her under the care of Mr Wallace with Mr Hamilton [Third mate] for the Sussias. A boat arrived, Mr Underwood in his new shallop from the Bonano's. Sailed the New England sloop for leeward. Dismissed the boatswain from his confinement, upon his submission and promise of amendment.

Sunday 28th October. Close rainy variable weather. At 10 this morning the yaul put back, Mr Wallace pretending she was too deep to go with safety, but beleive he hardly knows his own mind. Put his things on board Underwood's shallop, and brought the yaul alongside, and am resolved not to put it in his power to trifle with me again. Captain Ellis's longboat came in last night from the Bananoes with 8 slaves having been 4 days gone, and went away again this morning betimes. His doctor pretends that all the trade thereabouts is positively engaged to him, but I intend to try the truth of it.

Monday 29th October. This morning dispatched Mr Bridson [First mate] in the yaul with a letter to Mr Clow[6] at the Plantanes, who is the only person whose word I can place any dependance on, to know whether he can give me any encouragement to stay longer hereabouts. But beleive shall be forced to go from Captain Ellis wherever we meet, his large goldcoast cargoe enabling him to bear away all the trade here from a vessel that has only a common assortment. This day, however, I bought a fine man boy from Mr Langton, but the bars came excessive dear.[7] I likewise went on board the french vessels, who offered some fine slaves to sell for basts, nicanners, iron and knives, but was not able to come up to their prices, for they understood little of the trade, and are consequently extremely positive.

Tuesday 30th October. Variable weather, mostly a land brease, and in the night some rain with thunder and lightning. Have had no appearance of trade to day, the white men [resident European traders] being all exhausted, and I have not seen one Portuguese since I have been in the river. Have had Captain Cleavland's carpenter these 2 days to help finish our longboat, and hope to morrow she will be compleated.

Wednesday 31st October. Cloudy weather, a land brease all day and at 10 p.m. an exceeding hard tornado from the ESE. This afternoon arrived

[6] For Newton's previous contacts with Clow, see Introduction, page x.

[7] For trading by bars, see Introduction, page xv.

Mr Ord in a shallop from the Sussias with slaves. Went on board to make my necessary complements, but am of the opinion shall only get Mr Ellis's refusals, he having a great quantity of provisions, which are much in demand now, by being luckily timed. Hauled the longboat on shoar for the carpenter to put on a false keel.

Thursday 1st November. Fair hot weather, easy breases Easterly and calms. In the morning sent the punt on shoar with the carpenter, and the people instead of returning on board went to the french Scooner and got drunk; afterwards went on shoar to fight, which when they were sufficiently tired of, attempted to come off, but the ebb being made strong down, and they too drunk to pull well, came to a grapling amongst the rocks, so that when I sent Mr Marshall [Second mate] to them in Captain Ellis's boat, he was obliged to slip the rope, not being able to purchase it. I was unluckily by their means deprived of a boat when I wanted to go on board to see Ord's slaves, by which means Ellis got 5, being all that were worth chusing. Gave two of my gentlemen a good caning and put one (William Lees) in irons, both for his behaviour in the boat and likewise being very troublesome last night, refusing to keep his watch and threatening the boatswain. The carpenters fixed the false keel to the longboat today, but had not time to seat her. In the evening tryed again to get up the grapling, but in vain, so it must lye till I can bring the longboat upon it.

Fryday 2nd November. Fair weather, faint land and sea brease. This day paid the longboat's bottom with tallow, and in the evening brought her on board. I begin to be uneasy for my yaul; wait only for her, and to assist Captain Cleavland with my carpenter to calk his sheathing, according to promise, and in return for having had his all this week, and shall proceed down the coast immediately, for Captain Ellis gets all the trade that is stirring here, inspight of my teeth. Filled a boatload of water.

Saturday 3rd November. Fair weather, fresh land and sea brease. The carpenter finished his work on the longboat. In the morning had a visit from some Portugueese of Pirates bay, brought a woman slave, who I refused being long breasted, but dismissed them in very good humour with their reception, and they promise to bring me 2 young slaves in a little time. In the evening Mr Bridson came on board in the yaul, brought a letter from Mr Clow, denying that he had engaged any trade particularly to Captain Ellis. He saw Mr Tucker of Shebar at the Plantanes, who desires that I will send a boat to him, he having 8 slaves in the chain. By all I can gather there seems a probability of something to be done about Sherbro, so propose to lye a little time at the Bonanoes, and the rather as I hear that the *Ranger*, Coppal, is at Mana or Cape Mount, and the price of slaves thereabouts raised to 70 bars. Sent the longboat to weigh the punt's grapling, but the rope sliped being ill bent.

[Henry Tucker, mentioned above, was a mulatto. Many of the resident slave-dealers were mulattos, usually with European names – as Jemmy Cole, Will Freeman, and others referred to later in the Journal. Newton mentions two other Tuckers, John and Joseph, who may have been sons of Henry. On 10th December 1753 Newton writing to his wife calls Henry Tucker 'my friend Harry', and forty-three years later, when *Letters to a Wife* were published, he added a footnote: 'The man with whom I had the largest connexion in business and by whom I was never deceived.'

Nics Owen, in 1757, wrote: '. . . As I have nothing extraornery to fill up this part of the month I shall make up that by giving a charactar of a certain mallata man in these parts, who has acquired a great fortune by his skill and some other abillites in the way of trade. He commonly goes by the name of Henry Tucker and lives upon the same shoar as we do about a mile distant. He has been in England, Spain and Portugall and is master of the English tongue; he has 6 or 7 wives and a numerous ofspring of suns and daughters; his strength consists of his own slaves and their children, who has built a town about him and serves as his gremetos upon all occassions. This man bears the charectar of a fair trader among the Europeans, but to the contrary among the blacks. His riches sets him above the Kings and his numerous people above being surprized by war; almost all the blacks ows him money, which bring a dread of being stopt upon that acount, so that he is esteem'd and feared by all who has the misfortune to be in his power. He's a fat man and fair spoken, and lives after the manner of the English, haveing his house well furnish'd with English goods and his table tolarably well furnish'd with the country produce. He dresses gayley and commonly makes us of silver at his table, haveing a good side board of plate.']

Sunday 4th November. Variable winds and weather, and nothing remarkable.

Monday 5th November. Fair weather, land and sea brease. At break of day began to rig the longboat and put a cargoe in her for 18 slaves, but could not get her ready time enough for the day's ebb. Dispatched Mr Hamilton in the yaul for the Bananoes and Plantanes, and to watch Captain Ellis's boat. In the afternoon Mr Bridson went away in the longboat and anchored in Whiteman's bay to wait wind and tide to proceed to the Plantanes for a pilot, and from thence for Shebar. The carpenter at work on board Captain Cleavland. In the evening Will Lees petitioned to be let out of irons, and promising very fair with regard to his future behaviour, I thought it most prudent to try him, tho but for the consideration of our being a slaving ship, would have carryed him confined to the West Indies, as he first pretended to insist on.

Tuesday 6th November. Fair weather, land and sea brease. The longboat did not go out till this morning, which I wonder at, having had a fair wind and ebb tide in the night. At 8 a.m. Captain Ellis's longboat came in from the Plantanes, and went out again at midnight, Mr Tucker having sent exactly the same message to him as he did to me. I find whites, blacks, and mulattoes are all double and designing alike here. Sent 4 people on shoar to cut stantients and got off 2 boat load. Carpenter at work on board Captain Cleavland.

Wednesday 7th November. Winds and weather as yesterday. In the night came in Roger Edwards in a shallop from the northwards; find he has 9 slaves, 4 of which he says are a debt, and the remainder, I understand, he has privately engaged to my neighbour. Beleive I have lost the purchase of more than 10 slaves for want of the all commanding articles of beer and cyder, but cannot reckon my time spent here as wholly lost, as I could not have fitted my longboat so soon or so well to leeward. Got off two more boat load of stantients which think will be sufficient, and hope to be clear for sailing to morrow night.

Thursday 8th November. Fair weather, land and sea brease. This day bartered with Captain Powers for 110 gallons rum. Wrote to Messrs J. M. and Company[8] and put the letters on board the *Annapolis*. In the evening saw 2 large ships in the offing, sent the punt down; returned at midnight with an account that they are Dutchmen.

Fryday 9th November. At daylight unmored. At 9 a.m. came in the Dutchman, and a french built cutter in 6 weeks from London. At 11, being high water, weighed and worked down against the sea brease. . . .

Saturday 10th November. At 7 a.m. were about 4 leagues from the Bonanoes, at same time the yaul came on board, but brought no other trade than a tooth which [weighed] about 66 lb. But understanding there were slaves and Captain Ellis's doctor busy about them, and the people refusing to trade with the boat unless I came myself, hoisted the punt out and rowed in by about noon. Found that the doctor was flown with 9 slaves, but by the account of our people that met him afterwards, I do not envy him the purchase, 2 being fallen breasted women. Mr Wright shewed me 2 men boys which I may have on condition of sparing him some rigging for his shallop, but not otherwise. In the afternoon the vessel came in with the brease and anchored abreast of Mana's Port in 11 fathoms. At 8 p.m. I left the ship in Mr Marshall's care and went in the yaul to see what is stirring about the Plantanes. At midnight was about half way.

Sunday 11th November. By 9 rowed into the Plantanes, find the longboat has been gone into Sherbro 3 days. Passed the time till evening in hearing

[8] J. Manesty & Co., of Liverpool, the owners.

and telling news, not being customary to talk about business the first day [Sunday].

Monday 12th November. This morning Mr Clow shewed me 7 slaves out of which I picked 4, viz, 3 men, 1 woman. Payed what goods I had in the boat that were suitable and am to send the rest. In the afternoon weighed with the sea brease and ran half way to the Bonana's, then it fell calm and continues at midnight.

Tuesday 13th November. At daylight got on board. Went on shoar directly to look at 4 slaves of Chioa's, but they were all old. Went off again and put a fresh cargoe into the yaul. Left the ship about noon, Captain Ellis being just then coming into the road. Run with the brease to the Plantanes by sunset, delivered Mr Clow the remainder of his goods.

Wednesday 14th November. At day light weighed with the ebb and a land wind for Camaranca. At noon had the sea brease which ran us over the bar by 3 p.m.; rowed up the river, and at 8 p.m. reached the town. No trade here at present, but they promise to send a messenger immediately to Mr Corker, to inform him of my arrival.

Thursday 15th November. At 7 a.m. came away with the turn of the tide, got down upon the bar about noon, and was forced to anchor there, the sea brease and flood coming in together against us. At 6 p.m. weighed and steered over for the Plantanes with the land wind.

Fryday 16th November. At 4 a.m. anchored at the Plantanes. Found Captain Ellis there, and Mr Addu came down from Sherbro with 2 shallops. Cannot tell how many slaves he has, or whether any will fall to my lot or not, but he promised me a slave when we came to the Bonana's.

Saturday 17th November. Fair weather, land and sea brease. This morning Captain Ellis returned to the Bonana's, and in the afternoon Mr Hall came in his shallop from Sherbro.[9]

Sunday 18th November. This morning bought a manboy and a girl slave from Mr Hall, being all I could take out of 4 which he shewed me. In the evening weighed in company with Mr Clow and Addu in their shallop. When I was just upon the point of departure Will Lees attempted to leave me and hide himself on the island, and when I found him, he was very abusive, being drunk. Was obliged to give the blacks a gallon of brandy to secure him for me in irons, then took him into the boat and am determined to deliver him up to the first man-of-war I can meet. . . .

[9] Almost certainly Richard Hall, described by Nics Owen as a resident dealer on this part of the coast in 1753. 'This gentleman was one who has, like a great many others, spent his estate at home, therefore obliged to go abroad in search of a new one, one of those who goes by the general name of a good fellow, that dispizes all who shrinks his shoulders at that generous spirit of liberality, one who said in his hart "let tomorrow provide for it self" and to conclude he had a good many principles of honour, yet mix't with some stains that made his character jubus.'

Monday 19th November. In the morning had a smart SE. tornado by the help of which I got safe on board at 11 a.m. Found all well (thank God). The carpenter has finished the barricado, which I set him about when I went away.[10] Bought a woman and a girl slave of William Skinner, which he brought from Camaranca and 2 quintall of Camwood. Sent Mr Hamilton in the yaul with him [Skinner] into his river, he assuring me there is some trade there. I am informed that his Majesties Ship the *Surprize*, Captain Patrick Baird, is at Sierra Leon. In the afternoon went on shoar, but could hear of no trade. As I have great reason to beleive there will be a run of slaves from Sherbro shortly, and Captain Ellis proposes to sail in a day or two, I endeavour to wait with patience, for think it will be best to stay here as long as I am a single ship.

Tuesday 20th November. Fair weather, land and sea brease. Was most of the day on shoar attending upon Mr Addu, and am to have his answer to morrow, he not having yet settled with the frenchmen, to whom he says he owes 6 slaves. In the afternoon had a visit from Mr Clow and my quondam mistress P.I.[11]

Wednesday 21st November. Fair weather, fresh land and sea breases. In the afternoon, Mr Clow and P.I. being on board, one of their people, who had assisted me in securing Will Lees at the Plantanes, coming inadvertently too near him as he sat upon the windlase, he unexpectedly struck at him with the carpenter's maul, but just missed his head, the maul grazing on his breast. Had this been offered to any of the people of the main land or this island, it might have been of very dangerous consequence, but having P.I. with me, a laced hat made up the matter. Put Lees in hand cuffs and stapled him down to the deck, at which proceeding 2 others, Tom Creed and Tom True, behaved with a great deal of insolence, these three having been in a close cabal since the fighting affair at Sierra Leon. I bore it as well I could, being resolved to apply to the man-of-war to morrow.

> [From a letter to his wife next day: 'I have had a visit from my quondam black mistress P.I. I treated her with the greatest complaisance and kindness; and if she has any shame in her I believe I made her sorry for her former ill-treatment of me.']

Thursday 22nd November. At 9 a.m. set out in the punt with Will Lees in irons to deliver him to the *Surprize*, man-of-war, at Sierra Leon.[12] Had a

[10] The barricado shut off the slaves quarters from the rest of the ship. See entry of 7th December.

[11] See Introduction, p. x.

[12] H.M.S. *Surprise* and H.M.S. *Humber* were reporting to the Board of Trade and Plantations on the forts maintained by the Royal African Company and other traders.

strong SE. tornado all the way to the cape with hard rain and a great sea, that I was several times afraid that the punt would have filled with us, but by the favour of good Providence, got safe round the rock at 4 p.m., and on board the *Surprize* by 6. Waited on Captain Baird and discharged my man. Afterwards went on board the *Triton*, Boucher, lately arrived from Bristol. Arrived likewise since I sailed, a large cutter from London, Joseph Cockburn, master. No letters from home. In the morn the yaul came on board, brought 1 small girl which makes our number 13.

Fryday 23rd November. Fair weather, variable winds. In the morning waited upon Captain Baird to beg he would make the Bonana's in his way down to rid me of the rest of my mutineers, which he consented to, tho he did not otherwise intend to call there. He desired I would stay on board the *Surprize* to show him where to anchor, he having no body on board that was acquainted there. In the evening he unmored.

Saturday 24th November. At day light the *Surprize* weighed. I staid on board her till we came to the Bonana's which was about 5 p.m. Brought her to an anchor a little without our own vessel in 9 fathoms. Sent word to Mr Marshall to salute Captain Beard with 7 guns; he returned 5. Mr William Ansah Setarakoo, one of the African princes, as they were stiled in England, who is on his passage to Anamboo in the *Surprize*, came on board with me, and spent the evening with me very much to my satisfaction, being master of a great deal of solid sense and a politeness of behaviour I seldom meet with in any of our own complexion hereabouts. The first part of the night blew fresh with a short ugly sea; got down the top gallant yards.

Sunday 25th November. Fair weather. In the afternoon put 3 more men on board the *Surprize*, Thomas Creed, Owen Cavanagh and Thomas True, who all refused to sign receipts for their wages; delivered the bills for the balance due to them to Captain Baird and took his receipt. Entered 4 men he gave me in the room of mine, their names, William Lapworth, William Prickett, John Seringer and John Hymus. In the evening took Mr William [Ansah Setarakoo] on shoar to shew him the island, and [waited] on him myself on board the *Surprize* at night, where we parted both very well pleased.

Monday 26th November. Fair weather, land and sea brease. In the morning the man-of-war and the *Halifax*, Captain Ellis, sailed for to leeward. In the evening the yaul to the Plantanes to see if any trade is come down yet, and to inquire after the longboat, for I begin to be uneasy at her long stay. Filled a load of water. People employed, as have been several days past, in making waroning for a netting upon the awning. Carpenter at work upon the bulkheads.

Tuesday 27th November. Fresh gales of wind from the N. to the NE. with a great deal of rain. In the morning sailed the *Cornwall*, Duncombe, for to leeward. This day bought 2 men boys from Mr Wright. People employed as yesterday.

Wednesday 28th November. This morning at daylight had the agreeable sight of my longboat, and soon after she came on board with every body well, and brought 11 slaves, viz. 3 men, 1 woman, 2 men boys, 1 boy (4 foot), 1 boy and 3 girls (undersize), which makes our number 26, and likewise about a ton and half of Camwood. At the same time the yaul returned from the Plantanes, but brought nothing. Sent the longboat on shoar and the carpenter in her to repair. Were very busy all day rummidging and clearing the hold. Struck most of the dry casks, and drew off a pipe of spirits to make room. In the evening made an addition to the goods in the yaul to send her tomorrow into Sherbro in company with the longboat, Mr Bridson assuring me there is likely to be an extraordinary run of trade there and no competitors. Filled a load of water, and started into the empty puncheons between decks, then struck them all down in the hold.

Thursday 29th November. At day light the long boat came on board. Put another cargoe in her immediately, and about noon sent her and the yaul away together with a charge to keep together till they come to Mr Tucker's at Shebar, that they may both have the benefit of his protection, by means of a man he sent in the longboat, for while any of his people are with the boats none of the Sherbro men dare be troublesome. Carpenter building the after bulkhead of the men's room. Filled a load of water. In the afternoon went on shoar, but found no prospect of trade. Have expected Skinner these 2 days, who promised to return with 3 slaves, but shall not wait any longer.

Fryday 30th November. Bartered with a frenchman for 4 anchors of brandy. Bought about 13 cwt of rice of Maria's people. They brought a man slave on board, but it being late in the evening, they did not care to take the goods, but promised to bring him off betimes in the morning. . . . The carpenter finished the men's room, and began to build a place for the women to wash, etc., between the main chains and the barricado. Went on board the cutter who lately came in from London, and agreed with the captain to purchase teeth for him, and he to let me have all the slaves that come his way; his name, Cockburne.

Saturday 1st December. Very hazey weather. At day light hoisted the colours and loosed the topsails. Maria's people brought the slave off whom I bought, and, as soon as I left, the ship weighed, being just high water and a small air . . . at 3 p.m. being calm and flood tide, anchored . . . at 9 p.m. weighed again, but had very little wind afterwards, and at midnight is calm. Carpenter finished the washing place.

Sunday 2nd December. Hot hazey weather. At 2 a.m. falling calm came too again in 15 fathoms, and at 5 weighed with an air about NNE., which after sunrise freshened, finely steered out WSW. keeping upon the edge of St Anne Shoals. . . .[13] A schooner in sight all day to the Eastward steering our way. Suppose it to be Captain Bray of Bristol from Sierra Leon. This morning the moon was totally eclipsed, but the very thick haze hindering me from seeing the sunrise, I could not be so certain of the time to determine the difference of this meridian from London, as I was in hopes to have done. I perceived the shade enter upon the moon's disk about 3 minutes before 4 o clock, and it was wholly darkened by 5, soon after which lost sight of it in the haze, it being near the horizon. I had corrected the glass in the evening by the sun, but the only watch we have on board is good for nothing.

Monday 3rd December. . . . Carpenter employed in building the bulkheads in the women's room, gunner cleaning the small arms, and boatswain making a netting for the awning. . . . In the afternoon lost sight of the schooner, we leaving her fast, both by and large.

Tuesday 4th December. . . . Employed cleaning arms, making nettings, and carpenter closing up the women's room. By observation at noon was in 7°·41 which I may lay down as the limit of St Anne's bank to the Southward. . . . I reckon it a good course to steer from the Bonano's W. b S. about 14 leagues and then to hall round by the lead. I believe it runs out in a spit, and has not any thing like the breadth on the west side as represented in the chart. . . .

Wednesday 5th December. Hazey weather, a faint unwholsome land wind all day. At daylight saw the opening of Shebar to the eastward, we being about 5 leagues from the land, the wind being right off the shoar, and a SW. current, with a jumbling swell, could not get nearer, or even hold our own upon either tack, therefore came too with the coast anchor in 34 fathoms water, clay ground. . . . This day finished the nettings for the awning. Loaded the small arms. Carpenter compleated the women's room and fixed the bars on the gratings, which is a job I have long wanted done. . . .

Thursday 6th December. A continual calm. At 2 p.m. weighed with the flood tide to drive nearer the land, but at sun set can hardly perceive we have made any advance. . . . Hove a great strain to purchase our anchor, which we just saved, for found the cable broke about 16 fathom from the clinch, and upon examining, it proved quite rotten and bad. . . . Captain Bray and Captain Cockburne both in sight . . . and beleive they both intend calling at Shebar with me, but I am in hopes that my boats have before this secured a good part of the trade for me. Carpenter built the

[13] John Barbot wrote a few years before this: 'Take heed not to intangle yourself among the Shoals of St Anna . . . dead calms . . . are frequent here.' He mentioned that one English ship had 'spent five weeks in passing over them', and many vessels had been shipwrecked 'in the boisterous season'.

platform in the men's room, which has no lumber in it now but 6 chests of arms.[14] The ship is clear enough now to take 2/3ds. of our slaves without inconvenience; I wish one fourth of them were ready for us. Condemned 4 of the ship's small arms, being absolutely good for nothing, the worst I ever saw in my life.

Fryday 7th December. At 10 p.m. having shoaled our water to 15 fathoms, and being so near in as to hear the surf on the beech, came to an anchor with the small anchor, having spliced the cable anew and bent it again. Captain Bray about a league to the NE. which he gained upon us today in the little winds, our vessel requiring a fresh brease to make her steer. So I had the mortification to lye 2 hours with our head to the SW., while he was going his right course, tho we hoisted the boat out and did everything in our power to command her, but in vain till we got more wind. This day fixed 4 swivel blunderbusses in the barricado, which with the 2 carriage guns we put thro' at the Bonanoes, make a formidable appearance upon the main deck, and will, I hope, be sufficient to intimidate the slaves from any thoughts of an insurrection....[15]

Saturday 8th December. At daylight this morning perceived we were about 2 leagues from the land, and, very much to my disappointment, so far to the leeward of Shebar, that we cannot discern any thing of it. Weighed and stood up with the land wind. Passed Captain Bray who came on board of me, and is bound directly down the coast.... Reckon have gained about 2 leagues, and are yet 5 or 6 leagues to leeward of the bar. Must have had an extraordinary current when we were in the offing yesterday. Saw 2 lights on shoar in the night.

Sunday 9th December.... Anchored in 15 fathoms, the East point of Shebar bearing NNW., 4 leagues. An excessive high surf upon the shoar, which I beleive prevents the canoos from coming off. They make large fires in the night....

Monday 10th December.... At 9 came too off Shebar in 17 fathoms. Fired three guns and hoisted the Jack at the fore topmast head, the signal I appointed for the boats. Soon after perceived the yaul coming off; got on board at noon and brought a man and 2 boy slaves, No. 28 @ 30, being of Mr Bridson's purchase. Mr Tucker and the rest sending me pressing messages to come on shoar, I left the ship in the punt, ordering the yaul to stay on board till they heard from me, that I might not weaken

[14] The space between decks was five feet. The platform was a shelf dividing this space, but with a gangway down the centre. The slaves were chained in couples, right hand and right foot of one to the left of the other and so stowed upon the platform and the deck below – their headroom being rather less than thirty inches.

[15] Newton told a Committee of the House of Commons that when he was first mate in the *Brownlow* an 'insurrection' by slaves led to the death of one white man and three or four negroes.

our company on board too much. Got over the bar at sunset, not without some danger, the sea running high for so small a boat, and the ebb setting strong out, were a good while in crossing it. Got safe to the town at 9 p.m.

Tuesday 11th December. This morning I sent Mr Hamilton off to leave the punt on board and bring the yaul in with some few articles I wanted, to assort Mr Bridson, to send him to Jamaica [an African village on Sherbro island] for 5 slaves I had notice of. But to my surprize saw the punt returning again in the evening, and more so when Mr Hamilton informed me that the ship was gone, and that he had been at least 2 leagues to the seaward of where I had anchored yesterday, but could discern nothing of her. I was entirely unable to account for this unexpected accident; but being late, and the sea brease and flood hindring me from going over the bar, could do nothing but keep a fire upon the beach, in case they should have negligently let her drive with the land wind, which is the best I can hope for. Had a visit to day from the King of Charra, paid him dutys for the boats, and received 2 serevilas from him as a present, weight about 12 lb.[16]

Wednesday 12th December. This morning was down upon the beach by daylight with most of my own people and several blacks; but not seeing the least sign of a vessel, prepared to go out to sea to look for her. Got safe over the bar with both boats at 8, and at 10, having a good offing, anchored to wait for the sea brease, with which weighed at 1 p.m. and after running an hour down the coast, perceived her right to leeward under sail, and standing in for the land. About 4 she came to an anchor, and soon after we got on board. Found every thing safe, the whole affair being, as I suspected, owing either to sleep or negligence in not perceiving the ship drive the night I went on shoar, till she was in 20 fathoms water; and afterwards, attempting to regain her first place, the current carried them ferther to leeward....

['I leave you to judge of my anxiety....I put to sea with two boats which I had with me and after sailing some hours discovered the ship, when I was upon the point of giving up all hope of ever seeing her again.' From *Letters to a Wife*.]

Thursday 13th December.... Sent both the boats into the river, the longboat to go to Jamaica, and the yaul to lye at Mr Tucker's. Sent him the carpenter and taylor to oblige him to my interest if possible, for as I have staid so long to windward, would willingly compleat 50 slaves before I go down [the coast], and have great reason to expect to do it here in a few days.

Fryday 14th December.... Mr Tucker sent off a canoo to desire I would

[16] Some local rulers exacted duties according to the number of boats trading from a ship. The goodwill of these 'kings' was important.

send the punt in shoar for him, which I did, and he with Mr Cumberbatch [an African or mulatto] came on board to dinner, and staid all night. Bought 2 small girls of the former, 1 of 3 feet, and the other, 3 feet 4 inches, which make number 32. Agreed to lend them each goods for 6 slaves, to pay when I come up from to leeward: but beat their price down again to 60 bars, they having exacted 70 from Mr Bridson, and made them take a more equal assortment than they have hitherto done. Promised Mr Tucker the preference of my long boat when I go off, and he engaged to give me 6 slaves for her.

Saturday 15th December.... In the morning the gentlemen went on shoar. Sent Mr Tucker's goods in the punt at 2 trips. In the evening let go the best bower, and hove up the small anchor, found it foul, cleared it and then mored with a half cable each way. Engaged John Cumberbatch, a relation of Mr James, as a grimetar, to go in the yaul, at 3 bars per month, if he behaves well. At work rummidging in the hold, what leisure time we had. Mr Tucker sent me off a milch goat.

Sunday 16th December. . . . A canoe came off for Mr Cumberbatch's goods, and not being able to carry them all, sent the punt with her. When she returned, brought Mr Oborne off, who wanted to borrow goods for slaves; but gave him an absolute refusal, for do not think he is trustworthy, at least not as at present circumstanced. Am informed that William Cumberbatch and James Calker are at the bar with 5 slaves, and propose coming on board to morrow. Mr Bridson sent me a letter to let me know he was yet at Mr Tucker's, which I do not well know the reason of.

Monday 17th December. In the morning sent the punt on shoar with 6 casks to be filled with water; again the afternoon, and to carry Mr Oborne and bring off William Cumberbatch; but when she returned I found the King of Charra in her. Brought me a goat as a present, but was obliged to give him twice the value; saluted him with 8 guns. At noon the yaul came on board with Mr Cumberbatch, James Calker and John Tucker; brought off 4 slaves, 3 of which, 2 men and a girl, Mr Hamilton had bought, the 4th they brought to me, being a man, which I bought for 60 bars. They all begged hard that I would lend them for 5 or 6 slaves each, and seemed much displeased at my refusal. Our number is now 36. Mr Bridson sent me word that the blacks had plundered a french boat at Jamaica to her very sails and oars, which was the reason of his waiting to go down with William Cumberbatch, that he might protect him; but I depend more upon Mr Tucker than any of them, or should not trust my boat an hour in the river, for I beleive them to be all villains to a man except him. The french boat is come to his town this afternoon, with a mat for a sail and no provisions, but Mr Bridson supplyed them. In the evening the punt brought off 6 casks of water, and left 6 empty on shoar to be ready against the morning.

Tuesday 18th December. . . . In the morning sent the punt in shoar with the goods for the slave I had bought, and my 3 guests; she carryed 6 gang casks for water, but brought none off, the others not being filled. The mate of the Frenchman's longboat came on board to desire I would lend him a sail and a pilot to bring him over the bar, being in great distress, the boat entirely stripped to her bare mast, and no provisions, and 2 of his people wounded. He assures me that William Cumberbatch had a principal hand in plundering him, and as a convincing proof, showed me that one of the men I bought from him, he had purchased the day before he was taken, and I found that the fellow really knew him. He has lost about 800 bars, as appears by his invoyce. In the evening put more goods in the yaul, and sent her away with the land wind to Kittam, where the King of Charra is gone before to look out for trade for me. Having now 12 men slaves on board, began this day with chains and sentrys.[17] Discharged, cleaned and reloaded the small arms. About 10 a.m. departed this life Edward Lawson, who came out of the longboat when she was last on board, ill with a fever; this is the 7th day since he was taken: was obliged to bury him immediately, being extremely offensive.

Wednesday 19th December. . . . Sent the French mate on shoar, spared him provisions and lent him the fore top gallant sail, some small rope for rigging and one of the longboat's oars to help his boat over the bar, and sent the gunner with him for a pilot. In the afternoon the punt returned with 6 casks of water. This day cleared the women's room and scraped it.

Thursday 20th December. . . . Sent the punt for water; returned at noon with 4 casks, they having put the other 2 on board the french longboat, which we perceived coming over the bar about 1 p.m., but [it] was not able to get on board us, having hardly any wind and a strong ebb. Kept a light for them all night, and at 9 p.m. fired a gun. Halled the cables up, and scraped the boy's room, then quoiled them down again. No appearance of trade yet; begin to be tired of waiting here, yet know not where to go to mend myself, for if circumstances and probabilities may be allowed to guide at any time, it should seem reasonable to expect something worth while at this place, there being no ship between Sierra Leon and Mana, and the whole country in a flame of war.[18] Besides, by all accounts I can gather, this is the only place I can expect to lye a day without competition upon the whole coast, and here few ships are acquainted.

Fryday 21st December. . . . At daylight perceived the french boat on

[17] Asked by a Committee of the House of Commons if the men slaves were usually fettered, Newton replied: 'Always. I never put them out of irons till we saw the land in the West Indies. . . . It was the universal custom at that time.'

[18] Prisoners of war were sold as slaves. 'I verily believe, that the far greater part of the wars, in Africa, would cease, if the Europeans would cease to tempt them, by offering goods for slaves.' See *Thoughts upon the African Slave Trade*, page 97, below.

anchor about 2 miles to the offing, sent the punt with provisions and to tow her on board; brought her alongside at 10, took the people on board and sent her off to a grapling, for as she has no sails must be obliged to go down with me till they meet their ship, who the mate expects is waiting for them at Mana. In the afternoon sent the punt in shoar; she returned at dark, brought but 5 casks of water, the surf being exceeding high on the beach.

Saturday 22nd December. . . . Sent the punt for water; returned at noon with 6 casks. Mr Tucker came off in her and brought a tooth, weight 57 lb.

Sunday 23rd December. . . . This morning sent the punt on shoar with Mr Tucker; returned at 2 p.m. with 5 casks of water. At 10 p.m. heard three guns on shoar, suppose there is trade come down or the longboat returned from the Plantanes.

Monday 24 December. . . . Have been obliged to clear hause twice to day; the current, being very irregular, turns the ship round like a top. . . .

Tuesday 25 December. Heavy close weather, little winds away. Punt went for water, returned in the evening with 6 casks, brought off Sury Bombo of the Gallina's, P.I.'s brother, and a boy slave, 4 foot 3 inches. Can hear nothing of the longboat yet, begin to think her stay long, and indeed my own too.

Wednesday 26th December. . . . Paid Sury for his boy, No. 37, and sent the goods on shoar with him in the punt. He promised to return with 2 more, but failed as they usually do. Punt brought off 12 casks of water in 2 trips, and likewise the carpenter and taylor, for I propose to sail in the morning if no trade offers. Hear there are slaves at the Gallinas, but can give little credit to reports of any kind in this country.

Thursday 27th December. . . . At 4 a.m. unmored, and at 10 weighed. . . . Below the bar at sunset when, falling calm, anchored in 12 fathoms. . . . Scraped the quarter deck.

Fryday 28th December. . . . Reached Massa, a town in the lower part of Kittam, by sunset, then came to an anchor. Perceiving the yaul within shoar endeavouring to come off to us, the blacks making a great fire upon the beach, came too in 11 fathoms, about 2 leagues from the shoar. Fired a carriage gun, and hoisted a light for the yaul.

Saturday 29th December. . . . At 2 a.m. the yaul came on board, brought 6 slaves, 1 woman, 2 boys, and 3 girls, all small, No. 38 to 43. At daylight went to work to fit her out again, and sent her away by 10 to cruize hereabouts another week. Mr Hamilton informed me that he had met the *Adlington's* and *Hallifax's* boat, that the former ship had more than 100 slaves, but the latter had not purchased above 8 since she left us, that the *Pardoe's* yaul was lost here 4 days since, and he had bought 2 slaves that had belonged to them, and in fine that there were 16 sail of vessels lying at St Paul's when the *Hallifax's* boat came away. The boat preventing us moving with the land wind, were forced to lye till the sea brease came in, which was about noon. Had a fine gale till sunset, steered SE. along the shoar, and at 7 p.m. anchored abreast of Peter Tucker's town in 11 fathoms, they making a great smoke upon the beach.

Sunday 30th December. . . . Lay till 8 a.m. in expectation of a canoo, but nobody stirred. Weighed and at sunset came to anchor abreast of the Gallina's in 10 fathoms, the people on shoar making a smoak, but am apt to think they often do it on purpose to puzzle a ship. Fired a carriage gun. Saw a sloop rigged boat within us, standing up the coast.

Monday 31st December. . . . At 8 a.m. seeing no appearance of a canoo, weighed. . . . At 3 p.m. anchored off Mana in 16 fathoms, the high trees bearing NNE. In the road the *Hallifax*, Ellis, and 2 rum sloops almost slaved. Had a very discouraging account from them of the state of affairs to leeward, all about river Sestors being full of quarrels and palavers, and an epidemical sickness ravaging amongst the slaves purchased from thence; that the *Ranger*, Captain Coppel, was obliged to off before he had finished, having buryed 28 on the coast. Discharged, cleaned and reloaded the small arms.

Tuesday 1st January. . . . Tho I had little hopes of doing anything here against Captain Ellis, thought it proper to venture 1 day, to see if any thing offered, but no canoo vouchsafed to come on board. Am told that Mr Bryan is up in the country, and that he is indebted to these vessels as many slaves as can come down in a little time, and I am determined to lose no time till I have examined all to leeward. Wrote to Messrs J. M. and Company, by the *Dolphin*, sloop, Eson, who thinks to sail for Barbadoes in a week.

Wednesday 2nd January. Hazey weather. At 3 a.m. weighed with the land wind; at 10 doubled Cape Mount, about 3 leagues from the shoar. Spoke the *Pardoe's* longboat who is going to Kittam, and left their vessel at Rio Junck. Am afraid trade is bad enough there when they think it worth while to send their boats so far to windward. . . .

Thursday 3rd January. . . . Found we were off little cape Mount, and the french brigg at anchor there, that the longboat I brought from Shebar belongs to. Sent her on board. Had 8 or 10 canoo's on board to persuade me to anchor, but as I expect to buy rice cheaper below, and they had no slaves when the *Pardoe's* boat called here yesterday, I think it best to run down to Junck. The frenchman weighed with the sea brease at noon and soon overtook us, sent his boat to thank me for my trouble, and offered any payment in return. Perceived an English snow at anchor off little Monserada, run in and went on board her; prooved the *Africa*, Richardson, 9 weeks from Liverpool, has been 3 days on the coast, brought me a letter

* In the old-style calendar the new year began on 25th March.

from the owners. Halled up S. b E. to get round Cape Monserado.... At same time counted 7 sail in St Paul's road, and 2 more steering in. Am informed they are all frenchmen, but growing dark, could not distinguish their colours, 1 seemed a very large ship. At 8 p.m. took in small sails and clewed up the topsails in expectation of a tornado, but dispersed without hurting us....

Fryday 4th January. Hazey weather, wind down the coast, and mostly a fresh brease. At 2 a.m. doubled Cape Monserado; at 8 were abreast the little Junck. A canoo came off, but not promising any trade but rice, I would not stay. At noon past Rio Junque, a french ship and snow lying there, and at sunset came to anchor at Rio Grande Junque in 12 fathoms. . . . In the road the *Pardoe,* Anyan, of Liverpool, and a french snow; the latter saluted us with 3 guns, returned the like number. A canoo came on board; sent on shoar by her for my old traders to come off in the morning. The *Hunter,* Cockburne, at anchor close in upon the bar.

Saturday 5th January. Close weather with thunder, lightning and variable winds. At daylight had several canoo's on board, with traders to offer their service. Pitched upon Andrew Ross and Peter Freeman of King Andrew's side for my principals, and sent them on shoar with goods for rice, and to look out for slaves; on which errand dispatched 4 or 5 more with a whole bast and a large kettle each, to encourage the bush men. In the afternoon the yaul came on board, Mr Hamilton being very ill and not able to trade; brought a man and 2 small girls, slaves No. 44 @ 46. He says that business is likely to be pretty brisk at Kittam, but I beleive it will hardly answer to send so far. Have heard nothing of the longboat. Came down and anchored the french ship that we passed at Rio Junque. In the afternoon, the sea brease blowing fresh, the ship drove; let go the best bower, then tryed the small anchor with the punt, found it foul.

Sunday 6th January.... At noon, having intelligence of a woman slave on King James' side, sent the yaul in with the steward, but she returned in the evening without having concluded the business, the captain of the frenchman being on shoar, and determined to outbid every body, but as I understand she is a good slave, and he has no kettles, will have another tryal with him to morrow. At sunset rowed out the small anchor with the punt and mored. Bought a large canoo load of wood.

Monday 7th January. This morning went on board Captain Cockburne, he having told me he had 8 slaves to change with me for teeth and wood, according to our agreement at the Bonano's, but could not take them upon his terms, which was 60 bars per head round, tho there were but 3 sizeable and 2 of the remaining 5 under 3 foot 6 inches. Had a great deal of rain, thunder and lightning till noon, then clearing up. Sent the steward in shoar again in the yaul to purchase the woman slave, and brought her off in the evening, No. 46 [47]; she cost 63 bars, tho she had a very bad mouth. Could have bought her cheaper I think myself, but the trade is at such a pass that they will very seldom bring a slave to a ship to sell, and boat trade is not only dearer and more precarious, but generally helps a ship to ordinary slaves. Loosed and aired the sails, discharged and re-loaded the small arms.

Tuesday 8th January. . . . Put goods in the yaul and sent the steward in her to Little Bassa, Will Adams, the trader there, having come to me yesterday and offered his service, without which I should have been dubious, Captain Linnecar having had disputes with them lately on account of his yaul which drove ashoar there and was plundered. In the afternoon Ross and Free-man came on board, brought a parcel of rice and a man slave which am to pay for in the morning. Sent ashoar by the canoo 12 casks for water. The *Pardoe* sailed for to leeward. Tarred the sides.

> ['No one, who has not experienced it like me, can conceive the contrast between my present situation, distracted with the noise of slaves and traders, suffocated with heat, and almost chop-fallen with perpetual talking; and the sweet agreable evenings I have passed in your company.' From *Letters to a Wife*.]

Wednesday 9th January. . . . The traders came on board with the owner of the slave; paid the excessive price of 86 bars which is near 12 £ sterling, or must have let him gone on shoar again, which I was unwilling to do, as being the first that was brought on board the ship, and had I not bought him should have hardly seen another. But a fine manslave, now there are so many competitors, is near double the price it was formerly. There are such numbers of french vessels, and most of them determined to give any price they are asked, rather than trade should fall into our hands, that it seems as if they fitted out not so much for their own advantage, as with the view of ruining our purchases. This day buried a fine woman slave, No. 11, having been ailing some time, but never thought her in danger till within these 2 days; she was taken with a lethargick disorder, which they seldom recover from. Scraped the rooms, then smoked the ship with tar, tobacco and brimstone for 2 hours, afterwards washed with vinegar. Had some more rice brought off, to which with what came yesterday, amounts to about 1600 lb, and some fowls, etc. Canoo brought off a load of water.

Thursday 10th January. . . . Have heard nothing either of trade or traders today. About noon the *Africa's* longboat called on board in her way to Bassa, told me our own was coming. Saw her soon after, and at 4 p.m. she came to an anchor within us. Sent the punt and found them in a miser-able condition, having buryed one of the people. William Pucket, and Mr Bridson and the other 3 all sick, 2 of them dangerously. She brought 11 slaves: viz. 1 man, 2 women, 5 sizeable girls 1 boy and 2 girls small:

likewise about —— Camwood, 400 lb of rice, and a tooth, weight 32 lb. Mr B. says he has been 10 days from Shebar, and but for the assistance of the women slaves should never have been able to have reached the ship.

Fryday 11th January. Close dirty weather, wind down the coast and a great sea tumbling in. At 2 a.m. departed this life Andrew Corrigal, our carpenter, having been 10 days ill of a nervous fever; buried him at daylight, the 3rd in 3 weeks, and we have now 4 very ill. Came down the *Africa* and anchored without us; sailed past a snow and a sloop, both french. Brought the longboat on board and cleaned her, put more iron in for her ballast, and sent her to an anchor. Canoo brought off 2 load of water, and Ross the rest of the rice with what goods are left; find it stands me in near 10s. per cwt, and therefore shall buy no more, for can get it much cheaper to windward, where I beleive I shall be constrained to go in a little time, for trade seems as scarce here as there, and almost twice as dear. Besides that, having so many sick, am afraid shall not be able to keep our boats going, and they will not bring slaves off any where on this side cape Mount.

Saturday 12th January. . . . Filled 2 load of water and cleared the canoo, discharged my traders and put a boy on shoar, No. 27, being very bad with a flux. This day had another of our people taken ill with a violent bloody flux, have now 5 whites not able to help themselves. In the evening unmored and hove short upon the best bower.

Sunday 13th January. . . . Weighed with the land wind, steered downwards, about noon were abreast of Little Bassa. The yaul came off, brought 2 small boys; sent her in again with positive orders to buy none under 4 foot, for I think we have little ones enough, at the price they now bear. At 4 p.m. were abreast of Seventrees, and at dark anchored at Grande Bassa in 15 fathoms, the point of the beach bearing E. b N. Fired 2 guns. Buried a man slave (No. 6) having been about 10 days ill of an obstinate flux. The *Pardoe,* a french snow, and sloop here.

Monday 14th January. . . . This morning Yellow Will came on board; sent the punt in shoar with goods for 2 slaves on his account, and a few cloths to try the price of rice; she did not return till towards night. Got goods ready to send to Tabo-Caney tomorrow. Came down the *Pardoe's* longboat with 8 slaves from windward. Saluted Will with 3 guns when he went on shoar. The longboat lost her rudder in the night.

Tuesday 15th January. . . . At break of day sent the punt to Tabo caney with goods for 2 slaves to William Freeman. Sent 20 fathoms of remnants to Bassa for yams, palm oyl, etc. In the evening Yellow Will called on board to let me know he had a man slave on shoar for me. Made a new rudder to the longboat. The ship drove about 2 cables lengths with the sea brease, the coast anchor being rather too light, but did not let go the other, intending to birth anew in the morning.

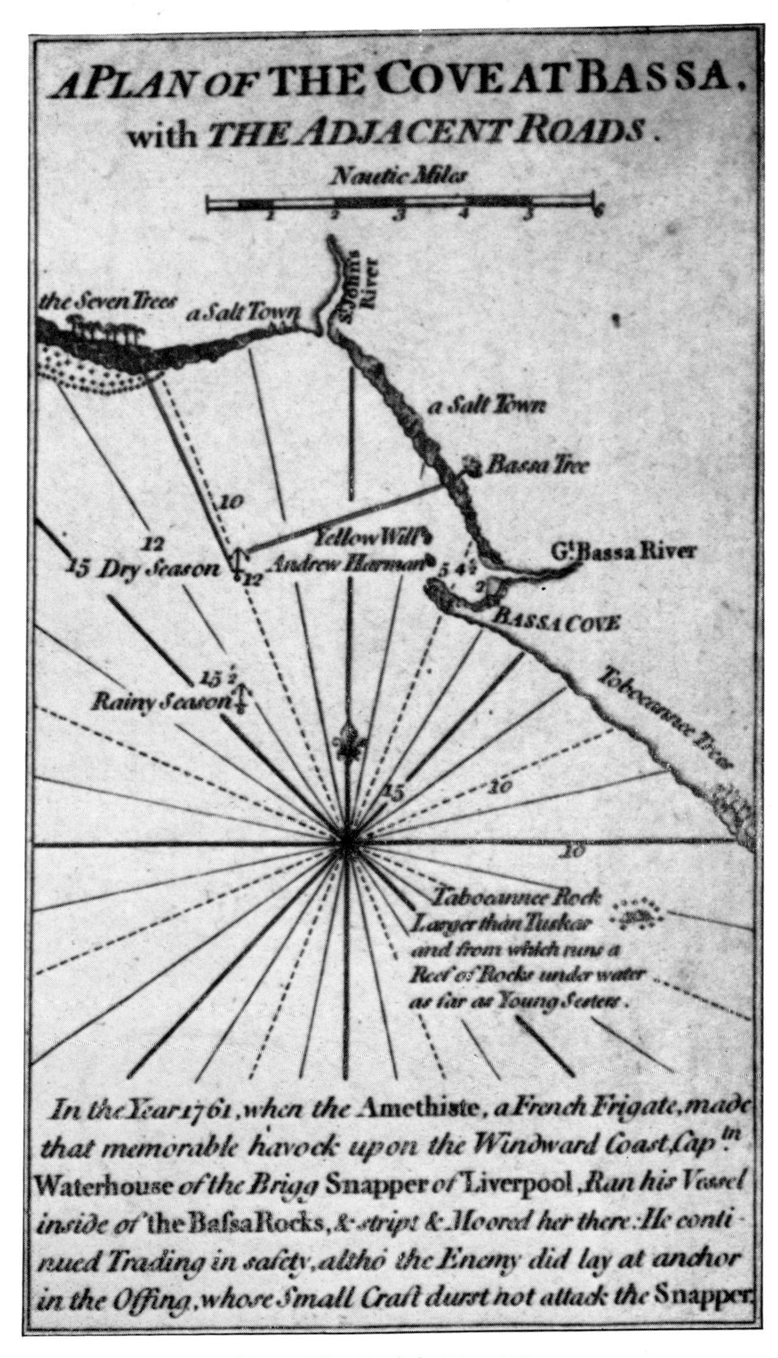

From *The English Pilot*, 1790

Wednesday 16th January. . . . At daylight weighed, run farther out, and came too between the *Pardoe* and french snow, with the best bower in 18 fathoms. Received a man slave and some yams and plantanes from Yellow Will, and a girl, 3 foot 11 from William Freeman. Sent Mr Hamilton in the longboat to Tabo-caney with goods for 2 slaves. The doctor having been ill these 2 days, borrowed Captain Anyon's to visit our sick people.

Thursday 17th January. . . . William Freeman came on board with a woman girl slave. Having acquitted himself tolerably, entrusted him with goods for 2 more. Yellow Will sent me word he had bought me a man, but wanted another musquet to compleat the bargain, which sent him. Had Captain Anyon's doctor again today. In the afternoon Mr Bridson had a relapse of his fever with a swelling and inflamation in his face. I thought him so well at noon that proposed sending him to windward in the long-boat in a day or two. The cook and 2 small slaves were likewise taken with fevers about the same time. The yaul came on board from little Bassa, the time I limited their stay having expired without 1 slave offering.

Fryday 18th January. . . . The long boat came up from Tabo-caney without doing any thing, the trader I sent her having never come near them after he went on shoar. Sheathed the fore part of the main mast and the deck between it and the barricado, and cased the pumps with sheet lead, that we may place the furnace amidships with security, which will give us a good deal of room, and we at length begin to have more mouths than our large iron pot can boil for. The *Hallifax* came down and anchored about Seven-trees. Have had no canoe of today either to us or the *Pardoe*, which I wonder at.

Saturday 19th January. . . . The *Hallifax* weighed and stood up the coast again. Yellow Will brought a man slave and took goods on shoar for 2 more, which is all I think to try for here, being so excessive dear, that I should be quite dissorted before I reach half my purchase. Received from him likewise 16 gallons of palm oyl, 4½ cwt of rice, besides yams and plantanes. Came down and anchored a french snow. Bricked and plaistered the furnace.

Sunday 20th January. . . . The French sloop sailed to leeward. A little before midnight, departed this life Mr John Bridson, my chief mate, after sustaining the most violent fever I have ever seen 3 days: had very little hopes of his recovery since he was taken on Thursday evening. I am afraid his death will considerably retard our trade, for I have experienced him very diligent and earnest in promoting the ship's interest, and always gained a great influence upon the natives wherever I sent him.

Monday 21st January. . . . At sun rise buried Mr Bridson. Hoisted the colours half mast, fired fourteen minute guns. Was employed most of the day in fitting out the longboat, put goods in her for about 15 slaves, for Kittam and Shebar under the charge of Mr Hamilton, to keep up our remembrance there and let them know that I intend following the boat as soon as possible, for if we cannot do our business there, I am afraid no other place upon the whole coast will suit. Yellow Will was on board in the afternoon but brought no trade.

Tuesday 22nd January. . . . No trade or traders to day to be heard of. In the evening came down the *Africa* from Junque and a ketch belonging to Cape Coast Castle called the *Pye*, master's name, Dun.

Wednesday 23rd January. . . . Yellow Will brought me off a boy slave, 3 foot 10 inches, which I was obliged to take or get nothing. Sailed a french snow downwards.

Thursday 24th January. . . . No trade today. I only wait the return of William Freeman from Tabo caney to bring me my 2 slaves, and would proceed upwards immediately, but have heard nothing of him since he went away, which is now a week. The trade has now come to that pass that there is no getting a slave without sending the goods first on shoar, tho by that step we hazard losing their custom entirely, as may possibly be my case; and the farther to leeward, the dearer and more precarious.

Fryday 25th January. . . . Yellow Will brought me a woman slave, but being long breasted and ill made, refused her, and made him take her on shoar again, tho I am not certain I shall be able to get one in her room. He brought of a cask of palm oyl I gave him to fill, containing about 50 gallons, and 30 fowls. Loosed and aired the sails; got up the spare sails out of the hold, and overhalled them, found the rats have done them a good deal of damage we being quite over-run with them and can not get a cat upon any terms, and these we brought from England have been dead sometime. Finished the platforms in the women's room and stowed the sails there for the present. Sailed the *Pye* for Cape Coast.

Saturday 26th January. . . . Nothing stirring from the shoar. The Africa's boat returned from Tabo caney with 2 slaves, and the *Pardoe's* without any. In the morning brought the yaul along side and took all the goods out of her but the iron, for am afraid I shall not be able to employ her again. Afterwards sent her to a grapnel, gave her a heel each way and scrubbed her bottom. Likewise hoisted the punt in and cleaned her. Had another white man taken ill to day, and one that was upon the recovery relapsed.

Sunday 27th January. . . . Yellow Will brought me a girl slave of 4 foot, and about a dozen fowls.

Monday 28th January. . . . In the morning scrubbed the bends. At 10 p.m. being calm, hove up the anchor, found the cable foul of the stock, cleared it, then towed out clear of the *Pardoe*, and came too again between her and the *Africa*. No news from Tabo-Caney yet. If I do not get my slaves before the next slant of wind and current offers to go up, beleive it will be best to sat down with the first loss, rather than spend more time to no purpose.

Tuesday 29th January. . . . In the morning sailed the *Pardoe* to Tabocaney. In the afternoon Yellow Will brought off a few returned goods. Came down and passed the French brigg that we left at Monserado. This day fixed the nettings upon the awning.

Wednesday 30th January. . . . The long expected William Freeman came on board and brought me a man slave. Went ashoar again and promised to return with another or the goods by the same time to morrow. The *Pardoe* weighed this morning from Tabo caney and worked up to Seventrees, having a small windward current.

Thursday 31st January. . . . Detected Will Lapworth, one I had from on board the *Surprize*, of breaking the lock of the state room scuttle and stealing brandy; put him in irons. Loosed and aired the sails. No canoo's off to day; will try them to morrow and no longer. The *Pardoe* has been in sight all day working off and on, and in the evening perceived another snow coming up from the leeward.

Fryday 1st February. . . . Waited for a canoo with a good deal of impatience, but in vain for none came off. If the opportunity continues, propose to sail in the morning, and rather, because the *Bridget*, Grierson, went past upwards to day and told the *Africa's* boat who went off to her, that the trade is entirely ruined at Rio Sestors, and the *Adlington's* longboat lately cut off there, the mate and 1 more killed. The *Bridget* lost her yaul and mate upon little Sestors bar, in short not a vessel that I speak with or hear of but has met some misfortunes, which ought to silence my complaints, who have hither to been exempted from any but the customary lot of mortality. In the morning William Lapworth confessed the fact I confined him for. Turned him out of irons and gave him a smart dozen for a *caveto*. At 10 p.m. a longboat came down from to windward but did not speak her.

Saturday 2nd February. Hazey weather. At 4 a.m. weighed with the first of the land wind which gave us a pretty good offing, about noon had the brease out of the sea, stood in, having a current setting in our favour, fetched within a league of Rio Junque by sunset, stood off an hour, then tacked and laid into the road, came too at 8 with the B.B. in 14 fathoms. The *Hallifax* and the *Bridget* here. Passed the *Pardoe* at Little Bassa.

Sunday 3rd February. . . . At sun rise made a signal for Andrew Ross who came on board and told me the slave I gave him to take care of (No. 27) was dead, which is indeed what I expected. As I had little prospect of doing any thing here, and a fine opportunity offering to get to windward, weighed again at 9 a.m., stood off till 2 p.m. for an offing, then tacked, being about 5 leagues from the land; had afterwards a very fresh sea brease and pretty far out and a strong current. Turned the yaul off with the steward and 2 hands and 1 boy slave to make the best of his way after us, she being very heavy to tow. At 5 p.m. passed Rio Junque, at 8 abreast of Little Junque, and at ½ past 10 doubled Cape Monserado as close as I durst venture having but 14 fathoms, stretched into St Paul's road, and just at midnight came to anchor with the B.B. in 13 fathoms. A large ship here within us. Mem. in the afternoon saw the *Pardoe* standing after us but beleive she anchored at dark.

Monday 4th February. . . . The ship's boat came on board, informed me that she was the *Indian Queen*, Rice, of Bristol, for Old Calabar, had been 6 weeks out. Have not had a canoo off today which I am surprized at. In the afternoon came down and anchored about I league above us His Majesty's Ship the *Prince Henry*, Captain Jasper. Saluted him with 5 guns, afterwards went on board him and informed of the French proceedings hereabouts, and the news I had at Bassa that 2 french men of war of 50 or 60 guns were gone down to Annamaboo upon intelligence they received that Captain Baird had sunk a small french vessel there, and that they threatened to send him to the bottom after her. The *Pardoe* came too without us, and the yaul came on board in the evening. Discharged and reloaded the small arms.

Tuesday 5th February. . . . Went on board [the *Prince Henry*] to see if I could get any hands from her, but there was only one offered who was a landsman, and, Captain Jasper insisting on my giving him full wages, I would not accept him as I am in hopes those we have now sick are all in a fair way of recovery. Put a cargoe for 4 slaves in the yaul.

Wednesday 6th February. . . . Had a canoo from Liverpool town,[19] trusted them with a few goods for rice to induce them to come off in the morning with a larger canoo to fetch our water casks. Sent the punt in shoar to St Paul's town to Peter Freeman; he promised to send a water canoo to morrow. In the evening sailed the *Prince Henry* for Annamaboo.

Thursday 7th February. . . . Will Grey of Liverpool town came off; entrusted him with goods for 3 slaves, to pay when I come down again, as beleive I must go up and down more than once yet. Loosed and aired the sails, smoked the ship with tar, tobacco and brimstone. Came down the *Brittannia*, Pemberton, of Liverpool, has 22 slaves on board and not a fortnight on the coast. Hove up the anchor to look at being clear, let it go again. No water canoo came off. Sent the steward in the yaul in shoar to look for trade.

Fryday, 8th February. . . . Will Purcell of Liverpool town came off and brought me rice for the goods that I gave him on Wednesday which turned

[19] An African village on St Paul's river. Also called Black Liverpool and Liverpool Beach Town.

out at 10s. per cwt, therefore I would have no more. With much ado persuaded them to take 8 gang casks in the canoo, sent the punt in with them with 9 more. In the evening they both returned full. Am obliged to give 2 fathoms of cloth and ten hand of tobacco for every trip. Being the time of making their plantations, they set a greater value upon their labour than usual.

Saturday 9th February. . . . A canoo brought a letter from the steward importing that he had done nothing yet at the town but heard there were slaves in the river if I would venture the boat in, which I sent him word to attempt, other ships daily sending, tho I look on the bar to be extremely dangerous, and the *Africa* had both yaul and punt oversat upon it when she was here. At 10 a.m. weighed and run a little nearer Liverpool town for the conveniance of watering. The punt made 2 trips to day and the canoo one, in all 26 casks. Sent some trifles to St Pauls for wood.

Sunday 10th February. . . . Got a load of wood off and sent the canoo again for more and 2 barrels in her for water. The punt and canoo made each 2 trips from Liverpool, in all 34 casks; one more in the morning will compleat us. Will Grey sent me off a woman slave with a young child, but I refused her, being very long breasted. The *Pardoe* sailed to windward.

Monday 11th February. . . . The punt and canoo brought off 17 casks which finished our watering. Had a load of wood from St Pauls. Discharged all the traders. In the afternoon the *Hallifax* came up from Junque. She ran under our stern; Captain Ellis gave us a What Cheer, then bore away and came to an anchor under the cape. Fixed a spar for a mast abaft and rigged it, fitted the lower steering sail to sat for a lug sail over the stern to keep the vessel too better in light winds.

Tuesday 12th February. . . . Weighed with the first of the land wind, stood up the coast; at 8 were abreast of little Monserado, saw 2 ships at anchor there which I take to be the *Triton*, Boucher, and the *Jason*, Gally, of Bristol . . . Mem: In the morning discovered the *Pardoe* standing up before us a great distance off, but by stretching farther out we got the advantage of the breases, that were within a mile of her at sunset, but know not which way she went afterwards.

Wednesday 13th February. . . . Had such a strong current off shoar that tho we steered mostly N. b W., which is 3 or 4 points within the land, could not get a distinct view of it, nor find soundings till 9 p.m. At 10 having 12 fathoms, bore away along shoar, and at midnight, the ground changing at once from hard sand to mud, came too with the small anchor in 13 fathoms, for fear a windward current should have helped us to Shebar, tho I should reckon we are 7 leagues from it, but being extream thick and dark, did not chuse to risque running farther. In the morning buried a boy slave (No. 66) who was taken ill with a violent flux the 3rd day after he came on board. Have 4 more ill but am in hopes of their recovery. At 9 p.m. fired 2 guns to let the longboat know we were passing if she should be about Kettam.

Thursday 14th February. A continual thick fog. At 7 a.m. weighed, the wind up the coast, run into 10 fathoms which was near as I durst venture, but could make nothing of the land, tho we saw the beach and breakers very high. Steered up along shoar about 3 leagues. At noon fell little wind; being afraid the sea brease should catch us too near in, stood out to 12 fathoms and anchored. Soon after the wind came right in, but very faint, and the fogg rather increased. Cannot see the land but by the noise of the surf must be very near it. Must wait with patience for clearer weather, for I neither know which way to steer, nor would it be safe to attempt it if I did.

Fryday 15th February. Faint land and sea breases, but such a thick fog that could not see the land. Did not attempt to weigh. Endeavoured to guess out an observation at noon, by which was in 7° 16^{m}, but cannot depend much on it, the horizon being very uncertain. Think, however, we can be but a little way from Shebar which I have formerly found to lye in about 7° 20^{m}. We have not yet found any tide, therefore I suppose we cannot have past it. Hoisted in the punt and coated her with pitch, tar and brimstone.

Saturday 16th February. A thick fog as yesterday. In the morning [weighed] and steered along shoar by the lead in about 13 fathoms while the land wind lasted. Could just see the beach but nothing more of the land. Reckon I run about 4 miles. At 10 a.m., the sea brease coming in, anchored, being afraid to keep under sail with us so near in, and was I to keep farther off should probably pass all. By observation was in 7° 17^{m}, but the horizon very bad.

Sunday 17th February. At daylight weighed with the land wind, the fog as thick as ever; steered upwards by the lead in 13 fathoms. At noon by observation had 7° 20^{m}. At 2 p.m. came too, having gone near 4 leagues as I reckon. Begin to be afraid I am past the bar, tho we have kept so near the land that I cannot conceive how I should miss. Have seen the breakers and the beach all the way, but nothing more. Propose to try with the boat to morrow if it does not clear up.

Monday 18th February. The thick weather still continuing, sent Mr Marshall in the punt to view the shoar. He returned in the afternoon, informed me we were about 2 leagues below the bar, that he had been at Mr Tucker's, who told him the longboat went downwards 9 days since with 4 slaves and every body well. Suppose I passed her at Kittam. The sea brease was too far down the coast to weigh after the boat came on board. Fired 4 guns while she was away.

On board the Duke of Argyle at Shebar. 1750

Wednesday ye 20th Febry fair weather, a fresh gale down the Coast at sunrise fird 2 Guns & hoisted the ensign in the FTG shrouds, in the Afternoon a Canoo brought Mr Marshall off. Mr Tucker sent word he will come off to morrow if he can, but now our Boat is gone, believe I shall hardly see him till the Yaul comes, to go for him

Thursday ye 21st Febry fair weather wind down the Coast, in the morning Mr Tucker sent a Canoo off with some fresh fish, & in the afternoon his Shallop wth a man & a boy slave & a Ton of Camwood in part of payment for the goods I left with him. The Schooner sails downwards she is from So Carolina, know not her name, one of her Commanders was on board me last night, & promisd to barter with me for a few necessarys, but as she is under the management of 3, I suppose the majority on board did not approve it. I own I think it more than one man can do at present, to determine on which part of this coast, the advantage of trade lies, but whether a Triumvirate will be able to manage better, time will shew.

69
70

Fryday ye 22nd Febry fair weather, land & sea brease, at day light saw the Longboat on shoar, came on board at 8, every body well, brought 5 slaves, viz. 2 men, 2 women & a small boy, a long months purchase. weighd wth the land wind & stood up abreast of the bar then came too for the sea brease, with wch weighd & run in abreast of the landing place, the bar just shut in, & the high trees NNE, anchord in 11 fathoms, am willing to lye as near the shoar as I dare, to encourage them to come off readily. Have seen the Yaul all day, but she could not get on board.

71 a 75

Saturday ye 23rd Febry at 3 AM the Yaul came on board, brought 4 slaves, 1 girl 2 boys & an old woman: at day light took the remaining goods out of her, pulld down her Quarter deck & wash boards, & fitted her with 6 oars to tend the Ships. At 10 Mr Tucker came on board, sent the Yaul on shoar, brought of Joseph Tucker with a girl 4 foot & a boy 3 foot 4 inches, bought them & sent the goods on shoar in the Yaul in the afternoon. Recd of Mr Harry a tooth wt 57 lb on account. Buryd a Man Slave No 33, having been a fortnight ill of a flux, which has baffled all our medicines. Put more goods & provisions in the Longboat & sent her away in the Evening for St Pauls, there being some encouragement there, & the Shebar trade seems quite exhausted —

76 a 79
80
81
M 5

Tuesday 19th February. Weather something clearer. . . . At 3 [p.m.] came too at Shebar with the B.B. in 13 fathoms, the high trees bearing North, a schooner at anchor ½ a league to the Westward, that came down from to windward this morning. Afterwards sent Mr Marshall ashoar to Mr Tucker's to stay with him till to morrow to enquire into the state of affairs. Punt returned at sunsett, and at 11 p.m. the watch upon deck, halling her up to bale, let her go adrift; got the ship under way as soon as possible yet not soon enough. The night being so dark, lost sight of the boat before we could cast before the wind. Followed her in the point she drove from us for about half a league, then came too in hopes we should perceive her pass us again; but in vain tho' we kept a strict watch for her. Had a heavy anchor down and a long scope of cable which made us some time in heaving up, and I was afraid to slip, not having a proper boat to bring upon the buoy, and might have possibly met some misfortune for want of the anchor before I could have got an opportunity to purchase it. I must now lye here per force till I see the yaul or longboat, and do business (if I do any) just as it suits the humour and convenience of the people on shoar who are seldom in a hurry. Patience! ————

Wednesday 20th February. . . . At sunrise fired 2 guns and hoisted the ensign in the F.T.G. shrouds. In the afternoon a canoo brought Mr Marshall off. Mr Tucker sent word he will come off to morrow if he can, but now our boat is gone beleive I shall hardly see him till the yaul comes to go for him.

Thursday 21st February. . . . Mr Tucker sent a canoo off with some fresh fish, and in the afternoon his shallop with a man and a boy slave and a ton of camwood in part payment for the goods I left with him. The schooner sailed downwards; she is from South Carolina; know not her name. One of her commanders was on board me last night and promised to barter with me for a few necessarys, but as she is under the management of 3, I suppose the majority on board did not approve it. I own I think it more than one man can do at present to determine on which part of this coast the advantage of trade lies, but whether a triumvirate will be able to manage better, time will shew.

Fryday 22nd February. . . . Saw the longboat in shoar. Came on board at 8, every body well, brought 5 slaves, viz. 2 men, 2 women and a small boy, a long month's purchase. Weighed with the land wind and stood up abreast of the bar, then came too for the sea brease, with which weighed and run in abreast of the landing place, the bar just shut in, and the high trees NNE.; anchored in 11 fathoms. Am willing to lye as near the shoar as I dare to encourage them to come off readily. Have seen the yaul all day, but she could not get on board.

Saturday 23rd February. At 3 a.m. the yaul came on board, brought 4 slaves, 1 girl, 2 boys and an old woman. At daylight took the remaining goods out of her, pulled down her quarter deck and wash boards and fitted her with 6 oars to tend the ship. At 10 Mr Tucker came on board. Sent the yaul in shoar, brought of Joseph Tucker with a girl (4 foot) and a boy (3 foot 9 inches), bought them and sent the goods on shoar in the yaul in the afternoon. Received of Mr Harry a tooth, weight 37 lbs, on account. Buryed a man slave (No. 33), having been a fortnight ill of a flux, which has baffled all our medicines. Put more goods and provisions in the longboat and sent her away in the evening for St Pauls, there being some encouragement there, and the Kittam trade seems quite exhausted.

Sunday 24th February. . . . Sent the yaul in over the bar to clean and fill water [casks]. The doctor went in her to Mr Tucker's to try if change of air and dyet will recover him from his flux, which he has been very ill of about a week. In the evening mored with the small anchor down the coast.

Monday 25th February. . . . At 9 a.m. the yaul came on board, brought 12 casks of water. At 2 p.m. sent her in again for another load, and to carry medicines to the doctor. Got up most of the beans from the starboard room, found them all very dry and good. Put the camwood that came last on board down there and the beans upon it.

Tuesday 26th February. . . . The yaul came on board with 12 casks of water. Mr Tucker sent me word that he will be off soon with some slaves, and that James Cumberbach is expected down to day from Diong. In the evening tripped the small anchor with the yaul and laid it farther in shoar.

Wednesday 27th February. . . . Sent the yaul on shoar to the beach, for Mr Tucker sent word that he was engaged and could not come off. Left a hand to cut wood. In the afternoon came down the brig *Mermaid*, Captain Keith, of Rhode Island, from Sierra Leon. He came on board and informed me that there had been many slaves there and no ship to purchase them for sometime, but the day before he sailed there arrived a snow from Bristol. The schooner people told me just contrary, that there were several ships and no slaves, or I should have been up there by this time. Got the rice up to air, and overhalled the larboard room.

Thursday 28th February. . . . Sent the yaul to the beach. Mr Tucker came off, brought with him 2 slaves, a man and a girl, which clears our account. Mr Cumberbatch is got as far down as Company's Island; suppose he will be here soon. Bought a hogshead of rum for Mr Tucker and some other trifles from Captain Keith. In the afternoon Mr T. went on shoar in the yaul.

Fryday 1st March. . . . Bought another hogshead of rum of Captain Keith and sent the former over the bar in the yaul to Mr Tucker. James Cumberbatch and Mr Hall came on board. Redeemed a free boy out of Captain

Keith for Mr Hall, that was carryed off last voyage to Rhode Island.[20] Paid 5 draughts of Camwood. Sailed the *Mermaid*.

Saturday 2nd March. . . . Mr Cumberbatch's shallop brought on board three slaves, a man, a woman and a small boy; took the former in part of payment, and bought the boy for 45 bars. In the evening sent the yaul to put him on shoar with Mr Hall who promises to be back with trade in 8 or 10 days, in which time I hope to see the longboat, and shall then (please God) try how affairs stand at Sierra Leon, but cannot leave this place yet. Mr Tucker's shallop came off; put goods in her to the amount, 800 bars.

Sunday 3rd March. . . . In consequence of this new account opening with Mr Tucker, he gives me the strongest promises that he will neither trade with any other ship, nor suffer anybody he has influence over. I have found more dependance due to his word than any of the white men hereabouts.

Monday 4th March. Winds, weather and business as usual. We continue to have the finest season that perhaps was ever known. It is with great regret that I see it running to waste but know no help for it.

Tuesday 5th March. . . . Sent the yaul for water, but there was so great a sea upon the bar that they durst not venture over. About noon had a good deal of thunder and the appearance of a tornado, but disperst. No trade, nor do I expect any till Mr Cumberbatch's people come down the River again, which I suppose will be in a day or two more, as he waits for them himself on shoar. He tells me that he shall have some slaves to sell, besides paying the 4 he owes me.

Wednesday 6th March. . . . Came up from to leeward and anchored near us a french brig that was at Sierra Leon with us. In the afternoon attempted to send the yaul for water, but the sea ran so high upon the bar, she was obliged to come back.

Thursday 7th March. . . . The sea running too high for the boat to venture over the bar, sent her to the beach for intelligence. Returned in the evening, brought word that Mr T. has 3 slaves for me, but they could not bring them off.

Fryday 8th March. . . . The french brig weighed to go into the river; sent the yaul at the same time. Both got safe over the bar with the sea brease, tho the sea seemed to run very high.

Saturday 9th March. . . . The boat returned, brought 6 casks of water and 6 slaves from Mr Tucker's, 2 men, 1 woman, 1 boy, 2 undersized girls, most of them brought to him for sale from the villains about Jamaica who

[20] Newton wrote 'Redeemed a boy slave', then altered 'slave' to 'free'. The incident supports, what Newton elsewhere asserted, that at this period the ships were careful to take only those who were already enslaved.

cut off the french snow, that has been some months in and about the river, a night or two agoe, and, I am informed, murdered the captain and every white on board; but expect particulars by next return of the yaul.

Sunday 10th March. At daylight sent the yaul in again for water, and with a few things Mr Tucker sent for. At 9 a.m. saw J. Cumberbatch's shallop come down almost to the bar, and then went back again. Suppose they were too late upon the tide.

Monday 11th March. Early in the morning saw the yaul and the shallop coming over the bar; before noon they came on board. The former brought 2 men boys and a girl (3 foot ten inches). In the latter came Mr Cumberbatch with 13, viz. 7 men, 5 men boys and a girl undersize. Received 4 men in payment of the money he owed me and bought all the rest, and a man and man boy from Joseph Tucker who came with him; in all 18, a very fine lot, but am sorry to reflect I owe it to another's misfortune, they being all the Frenchman's slaves, and I am well assured that these two were the principals in taking the vessel, but am obliged to dissemble at present and say little, or hurt my own business without any advantage to the sufferers. Since it is done I would get as many of their slaves as I can, and expect the rascals will bring me more shortly if I do not affront them. Mr Tucker sent me likewise 13 quintall of camwood. The doctor came on board.

Tuesday 12th March. . . . Was busy the whole day in paying for my yesterday's purchase. Lent Cumberbatch and Jo. Tucker each goods for 2 slaves to induce them to come again. Sent the yaul to the beach, brought of Mr Henry Tucker, who informed me of the whole affair, and confirmed that these I am obliged to trade with were the first in the enterprize, tho they had no quarrel or dispute with them, but meerly for the sake of plunder. The French captain is living and Mr Tucker has redeemed him from the natives, but they murdered 6 of the people and drove 3 overboard.

Wednesday 13th March. . . . Sent the yaul over the bar. A ship passed us in the offing steering downwards, shewed no colours. Cleaned and reloaded the small arms. Mr Marshall was taken of a fever on Sunday morning, was afterwards better, but to day relapsed again. Have likewise 2 slaves ill of the same disorder.

Thursday 14th March. . . . The yaul came on board with 12 casks of water, sent her away again at 10, but the sea ran too high to venture the bar, so was obliged to come back again. Unbent the sails to tar the yards, found them all more or less damaged by the rats. Mended the fore topsail. Tarred the bowspreet and yards forward.

Fryday 15th March. . . . Tarred the after yards and mended the foresail and maintopsail. I find I have kettles for about 40 slaves yet, besides what are already paid for, and not received, in number about 12, and exclusive of the longboat.

Saturday 16th March. . . . The yaul attempted to come out, but the bar being bad she put back again. . . .

Sunday 17th March. . . . The yaul came on board with 6 casks of water. Saw a sail to leeward. . . .

Monday 18th March. . . . Mr Tucker came on board, brought with him 2 slaves, a man boy and a woman. The sail we saw yesterday came in with the sea brease and anchored near us, is a schooner named the *Brittania*, Thurston, Master. By him understand that the *Triton*, *Pardoe* and *Brittania* snow are at St Pauls, likewise the *Floramel* who is just come up from Settra Crue, and brought few more slaves than she carried down. In the afternoon sent the yaul on shoar with Mr T.; landed 4 people to bring his shallop, he having lent her to me to get water, as the bar is so inconvenient for our own boat.

Tuesday 19th March. . . . Come up from to leeward the *Rebekah*, sloop, William Williams, of New York. Bought a hogshead of rum of Captain Thurston which I am obliged to do, tho have a great deal of my own brandy unsold, to keep the trade in my hands; for the people will have rum from somebody while [it is] to be got. Spared him 3 casks of water. In the afternoon he weighed and went down again, for Mr Tucker, according to his promise to me, would not give him the least in encouragement to stay. The shallop brought 12 casks of water; sent her in again.

Wednesday 20th March. . . . Went on board the sloop, bought a cask of pork for Mr Tucker, who came on board about noon with 4 slaves, 2 men, 1 woman girl, and 1 woman with a small child; settled accounts with him and paid him the balance. I am now again, as formerly, much disconcerted by the tedious stay of the longboat. I limited her to 3 weeks, and had she returned in time, could have got several slaves in the river, but she has been a continual hindrance to me rather than a help the most part of the voyage.

Thursday 21st March. . . . Loosed and aired the sails. In the afternoon the shallop brought on board 16 casks of water; sent her in again.

Fryday 22nd March. . . . Exchanged with Captain Williams No. 60, 61; 2 small boys (of 3 ft 4 in) for a girl (4 foot 3 in) and No. 80, a small boy (3 ft 8 inches) for a woman, he being only for small slaves. About noon he sailed for Sierra Leon.

Saturday 23rd March. . . . The shallop brought 16 casks of water; sent her in again. I understand by the people who all begin to think the longboat stays long, that Mr Hamilton shot a man last trip somewhere below Cape Mount, but I never heard a word of it till today. If I had known it at first, should not have sent her down there again, nor any where else in his charge. But I begin to fear they have either surprized or over powered him out of revenge, for unless first provoked, I am well assured, the natives are not inclined to quarrel on this side Rio Junque, and I ordered him not to pass Cape Monserado.

Sunday 24th March. The first part fair, the latter cloudy weather inclining to rain, winds as usual. Nothing more remarkable.

A.D. 1751

Monday 25th March. . . . The shallop brought off 16 casks of water; sent her away again immediately to save tide in. Samuel Skinner came over the bar in a canoo and brought me 2 fine slaves, a woman and a girl (of 4 foot). As this is the first black man's trade I have had here, endeavoured to please him in hopes he may induce others to come.

Tuesday 26th March. . . . The shallop came down to the bar this morning but was obliged to go back again, there being a great sea and (at that time) no wind. Mr Tucker sent word by a canoo that he would be off in the morning.

Wednesday 27th March. In the morning had a hard tornado from the ESE. with much rain; cleared up 10 a.m. Sent the boat in shoar for Mr Tucker; came off at noon, brought with him a man boy slave. The shallop was down upon the bar but could not get over, the sea running very high. In the evening sent Mr Marshall on shoar to go in a canoo of Mr T. to the Plantanes to remind Mr Hall of paying me for redeeming his boy, for it is now double the time in which he promised to come. Sent likewise a letter to Mr Clow to beg it as a great favour (necessity dictating) that he would sell me a few slaves to forward me off the coast. Our slow purchase and the pressing season reduces me to court those whose behaviour I have reason to resent and despise.

Thursday 28th March. . . . At 10 a.m. saw the longboat with as much surprize as pleasure, for I had quite given her up. At 2 p.m. she came on board, brought 7 slaves, 1 man, 2 women, 1 boy (4 feet 2 inches) and 3 small boys. Mr Hamilton excused his long stay on account of a general sickness which seized them in St Paul's river. He and two of the people are pretty well recovered, but the other two are extreamly ill, one indeed seems at the point of death. Brought likewise about 8 cwt of rice.

Fryday 29th March. . . . Took all the goods and stores out of the longboat, cleaned her and mored her, and shall deliver her up to Mr Tucker when he comes off, for such long voyages and small returns are not worth sending her away for, and she never has come on board yet without bringing sickness. At 5 a.m. departed this life Thomas Bridson, ship's apprentice, one of the two that came yesterday in the boat; am in hopes the other is in a way of recovery. No news from the shoar today.

['I give and take a good deal of raillery among the sea captains I meet with here. They *think* I have not a right notion of life, and I *am sure* they have not. They say I am melancholy: I tell them they are mad. They say, I am a slave to one woman, which I deny; but can prove that some of them are mere slaves to a hundred. They wonder at my humour; I pity theirs. They can form no idea of my happiness; I answer, I think the better of it on that account; for I should be ashamed of it, if it was suited to the level of those who can be pleased with a drunken debauch, or the smile of a prostitute. We shall hardly come to an agreement on these points; for they pretend to appeal to experience against me'—From *Letters to a Wife.*]

Saturday 30th March. . . . A very high sea upon the bar, as has been all this week; have not seen the shallop attempting to out since Wednesday. Mr Tucker's people carried the canoo from the beach which I wonder at.

Sunday 31st March. . . . Saw the shallop coming out, but it fell calm before she reached the bar. The tide, which now at the springs runs very rapid and sets over the banks, constrained them to anchor, and the sea brease came in late, that they had not time to work over before the flood met them and carried them up again. . . .

Monday 1st April. . . . A high sea upon the bar which prevented the shallop coming over tho she was down again. Sent Mr Hamilton to bring her out. When the yaul returned, brought off Mr Tucker who stayed on board all night. Agreed with him to leave 1000 bars in his hands, besides the longboat, till I return from St Pauls where I propose to go in a few days to rice and water, for we cannot be supplyed with either hereabouts according to our expence [i.e. consumption]. I cannot properly call this lending him money, for I am, rather, obliged to him to take it.

Tuesday 2nd April. At 3 a.m. had a tornado up the coast which blowed extreamly hard for about an hour with heavy rain; started the small anchor almost home to the other. In the forenoon hove them both up and mored anew and more athwart, the best anchor in shoar, and the small one to the SW., for have need of both to bear in these violent squalls. Delivered up the longboat to Mr Tucker's people and put most of the 1000 bars in her. I agreed with him at first to pay 6 slaves for her conditionally that she should be rendered to him without damage, but partly because her bottom is much eaten by the worm, and partly in acknowledgement of his behaviour in assisting me with all his interest here, I have consented to take 5.

Wednesday 3rd April. . . . Put most of the remaining goods into the longboat and sent her in. At noon the shallop came off, after being detained 11 days by the high sea upon thc bar. She was not able to fetch us, came too in shoar. The yaul made 2 trips for the 17 casks of water and 4 cwt of camwood and some rice, which Mr Tucker sent for half a tun, but turned out no more than 7 cwt by my measure. Whether his or mine is wrong, or whether the difference is owing to waste in the shallop, I cannot tell; but probably the latter for it has been on board her a week.

Thursday 4th April. . . . At 4 a.m. the yaul filled astern and before we could get her alongside, overset. It was with a great deal of difficulty that we saved her, got the tackles on and hoisted her in upon deck, almost stove in pieces, but lost everything out of her, the rudder, mast and sail and 5 oars and a large graplin and rope. Repaired her as well as we could and turned her out again and sent her to the beach perceiving a smoke. Fitted her with the punt's oars and two broken ones belonging to the longboat. Going on shoar they picked up two more and the mast and sail. Mr Marshall came off in her, brought me the same boy from Mr Hall that I redeemed, he not being able to pay 2 slaves for him, tho he talked as if he was master of 20 when on board. Mr Clow answered my letter and says he will send me 5 slaves at 75 bars per head, which I allowed Mr Marshall to offer rather than lose his trouble: so I shall not think myself obliged to him at all if he sends, but beleive I shall sail before his boat comes. James Cumberbatch's shallop is at last come down with 4 or 5 slaves and I expect him on board to morrow.

Fryday 5th April. . . . Loosed and aired the sails, and likewise overhalled and aired the spare sails, found them much damaged by the rats, but know no help for it; stowed them away in the store room. In the morning sent Mr Hamilton in the shallop to return her to Mr Tucker, and in the afternoon sent the yaul to the beach to bring off our people, came back a sunset. I understand Cumberbatch is not yet come down, and Mr Osborne is afraid to bring the slaves on board without him lest I should detain all together. A guilty conscience haunts them all – they would willingly cheat me, but are afraid of being known to be what they are.

Saturday 6th April. . . . Towards midnight had a very long hard tornado from the SE., but not much rain, could save only 2 casks of water. Overhalled the rice rooms thoroughly and found some of the pease quite spoilt, tho no wet had come near them, condemned about 10 bushels. Have about 15 days rice on board, but expend our water so fast that I must go down. We have now 9 buts empty in the ground teer. In the afternoon sent the yaul in shoar, brought off a girl slave from Mr Tucker of 4 foot. Buryed a man boy (No. 110) the only one we have lost the 2nd time the flux as been amongst us. We have had about 12 ill but all I hope recovering.

Sunday 7th April. . . . Mr Tucker came off and brought two of his wives, his sister and a daughter of Mr Obvian's with 3 female attendants, who are to be my passengers down to Mana, which he looks upon as a mark of his particular confidence in me, but I would have been glad to decline the honour, but as I have been much obliged to him on the ship's account, and expect farther service from him yet, I durst not refuse. Mr Cumberbatch came on board, paid me a woman and a boy (4 foot 1 inch) for his debt, and sold me 2 boys (of 3 ft 10 inches each). He had an old man but I would not buy him. Mem: he owes me still 26 bars. Our longboat (or rather now Mr T.'s) came out and he sent her away down towards Mana before us that I might not be detained there. Two of Mr Obvian's shallops are going down with us likewise.

Monday 8th April. . . . Sent the yaul in shoar with the gentlemen, and when she returned hoisted her in. Weighed with the first air of the sea brease. . . . It proved but faint all day, and at sunset came up the coast again. Came too with the B.B. in 16 fathoms about 5 leagues below the bar. Had a great deal of lightning all the evening, expected a tornado but proved nothing, or past us. The 2 shallops anchored near us.

Tuesday 9th April. . . . Both land and sea brease proved very indifferent. At sunset were 2 leagues short of Peter Tucker's town. Kept under easy sail.

Wednesday 10th April. . . . At daylight found we were but abreast of the Gallinas, having had a windward current. At 8 a.m. calmed. At 10 the sea brease came in, but was soon overpowered by a smart tornado which obliged us to furl all and come to anchor in 25 fathoms, for we are so very light that I am afraid to venture her broadside to the wind, the squalls generally blowing excessive hard. Saw our old longboat steering out of the sea, but could not perswade them to come on board by all the signals I could make. At 4 p.m., weather something settled and wind down the coast, weighed but in an hour's time it came off the land so far that I found we drove fast out; came too again in 20 fathoms with the small anchor.

Thursday 11th April. . . . Fired 3 shot at the longboat to make her come on board that I might put my passengers in to make the best of their way (for I begin to be heartily tired of their company) but being out of reach they went on before us and weathered P.I.'s point which we could not do. Filled 8 buts of salt water.

Fryday 12th April. . . . With the sea brease stretched into Mana road, anchored with the B.B. in 16 fathoms. The schooner that was at Shebar with 3 commanders here. Saw a ship standing out of Cape Mount Bay which knew to be the *Triton*, Boucher. At sunset his longboat came on board to borrow some shot, for he expended his stock this morning in a skirmish with a french brig that lies at the cape: but he sent to the wrong vessel for we have not 30 on board and those all swivels.

Saturday 13th April. . . . At daylight sent the yaul in shoar with my lady passengers, and luckily a canoo came off immediately and rid us of them. Bought 5 slaves today from 2 blacks, 1 man, 1 man boy, 1 boy, 1 girl (4 foot) and 1 boy (3 feet 7 inches). Borrowed a canoo from the schooner to carry goods and traders on shoar. Captain Boucher and the French brig have been at fox and goose chase all day, the latter going incomparably well made her own diversion; she stretched past us to view us, and I suppose knew us to be the vessel that saved his longboat for him. At night they both stood into the bay and anchored again, Boucher close in shoar and the frenchman a league without him....

Sunday 14th April. Very unsettled weather with a great deal of rain; could not weigh all day, the wind being no better than SW. till 5 p.m. when backed in a hard squall to West. Took the advantage of it and weighed immediately, was obliged to carry a very prest sail to keep off, the current being very strong upon the land. I found the ship very much stiffer than I expected, but I should not have tryed her so far but that we are very short both of provisions and water, and it would be of very bad consequence to be detained hereabouts a week longer, for we can get neither. Run over within a league of Cape Mount then the wind came so far forward that I was afraid I could not double it, and, as there is no anchoring between the points and likely to be calm, I bore away for the french brig, and at dark came too just within him in 20 fathoms....

Monday 15th April. . . . The french brig weighed with us. At noon doubled Cape Mount. Left the *Triton* and Captain Thurston in the bay. Had a fine brease till dark, but afterwards little wind, but a great deal of lightning and black threatning clouds all round....

Tuesday 16th April. . . . At noon were abreast of Little Cape Mount. Had a windward current all day, but the sea brease proved favourable, steered along SE. b E. and at 8 p.m. anchored in St Paul's road with the sheet anchor in 14 fathoms. Found our old companion the *Pardoe* here, and got from her some long expected letters from home that came on the coast in the *Adlington*, and have since been transported into 5 or 6 different vessels. News by Captain Anyon as follows: Captain Wainwright of the S & N dyed here and was buryed, and the snow sailed yesterday. Ellis and Grierson are gone down the Gold Coast, the latter with 150 slaves, the former 170; Linnecar, 140, not yet gone off. Pemberten has lost his longboat with goods for 14 slaves, run away with by his people – they made bold with his punt the same way about 6 weeks ago. Richardson has had his doctor stopt 3 weeks, and redeemed at a great price at Rio Sestors; and finally a french snow cut off at Grande Bassa.

Wednesday 17th April. . . . At daylight made our signal for traders. At 8 a.m. Peter Freeman came on board and was soon followed by several others. Engaged the most of them, and disperst them on shoar with goods, some for rice, others for wood, etc. They promised to send a water canoo but omitted it. Sent Mr Hamilton on shoar to stay at the town to *reconnoitre*. Borrowed some rice and wood of Captain Anyon, for present expence having so nicely guessed our provisions as it happened, that we brought only one meal here with us; for I was not willing to purchase when I was here before because I expected and was promised to be supplyed at a cheaper rate from Sherbro.

Thursday 18th April. . . . In the morning veered the sheet cable out to the bare end upon deck and let go the B.B. to the Westward and mored. Hired more traders and canoos; got off one load of wood and 12 casks of water and about 160 lb rice. Buryed a woman slave (No. 127) of a flux.

Fryday 19th April. . . . Had a very busy day between attending the canoos and clearing the hold. Got off 5 load of wood and 3 of water, containing 32 casks which filled almost 3 buts, beside our expences. Began to raise the water casks we stove at the Bananoes, and to pump out the salt water we lately filled in the ground tier.

Saturday 20th April. . . . The canoos brought us 5 load of wood and 32 casks of water, filled about 2 buts besides expence and filling up those that have leaked in the ground tier. Mr Hamilton came on board, brought about 420 lb rice; sent him on shoar again with some more goods. Cooper at work raising and overhauling water casks. Came down and anchored within us the *Triton*.

Sunday 21st April. . . . Was obliged to wave the consideration of the day [the religious service for the crew] for the first and, I hope, the last time of the voyage, the season advancing fast and, I am afraid, sickness too; for we have almost every day one or more taken with a flux, of which a woman dyed to night (No. 79). I imputed it to the English provisions and have given them rice twice a day ever since I came here; a little time will show whether it agrees better with them than beans or pease. Started all our bread into the bean room, and the cooper prepared 5 of the 7 buts for water. The canoos from St Pauls brought off 24 casks of water and 5 load of wood. A canoo of Liverpool town that had 8 of our casks was stove last night going on shoar. They say they have saved the casks but I must send the yaul for them, they not having a canoo fit to bring them off. One [of] my traders brought about 300 lb rice. Captain Anyon discharged his trader, William Purcell of Liverpool; he came to me and I gave him some goods for rice for his former good behaviour and to encourage him to procure my 3 slaves that William Grey owed me, who dyed soon after I went to windward. He assures me I shall have them in a few days.

Monday 22nd April. . . . Sent the yaul to Liverpool for the water. She returned at noon, but the St Paul's canoo only made one trip to day, so that we saved little more than a but. Canoos brought on board 2 load of wood and about 2000 lbs of rice from different quarters. In the night a woman slave dyed of a flux (No. 112). Cooper at work upon the water casks.

Tuesday 23rd April. . . . Made 2 trips to day with the yaul for water and rice. Canoo's brought of 3 load of wood; sent the largest of them with three barrels. The St Paul's canoo likewise came twice. So that on all hands filled more than 4 buts and got on board about 3800 lb of rice, dry and in good order. The *Pardoe* sailed in the morning bound down the Gold Coast, but, the wind being far up and a very strong windward current, gained no ground all day. Sent a girl, ill of the flux (No. 92) on shoar to Peter Freeman, not so much in hopes of recovery (for I fear she is past it), as to free the ship of a nuisance. Cooper finished all the casks. Mr Hamilton came on board sick.

Wednesday 24th April. . . . A squall about noon frightened the water canoos from coming off a second time. Made one trip with the yaul, got off in all 2 buts of water, 2 load of wood and about 850 lb of rice. The *Pardoe* in sight all day, got nothing but an offing. The yaul brought word that the girl I sent on shoar yesterday very ill of a flux, dyed this morning. I have had 5 slaves taken with the same disorder within these 2 days, but am unable either to account for it or to remedy it.

Thursday 25th April. . . . The *Pardoe* in sight all day, in the evening stretched in and anchored less than a mile from where she first weighed. Loosed and aired the sails. The large canoo made 2 trips and the small one and yaul each 1 for water. Filled about 3 buts and ½ besides expence. Canoos brought off 4 load of wood and about 3600 lb of rice. Sent a few more goods on shoar.

Fryday 26th April. . . . The yaul and canoos made each 1 trip, filled about 2 butts, received about 2 load of water and 1600 lb of rice. In the evening came up and anchored the *Africa* from Rio Junque. Captain Richardson came on board and confirmed the indifferent account I have heard of affairs to leeward; he has purchased about 80 slaves of all sizes, buryed his doctor and 7 more whites. He says Captain Freeman lost his longboat a few days agoe in the same manner as Pemberten did, as likewise Wainwright's yaul. It is odd that 3 sucessive vessels should all bring piratical crews.

Saturday 27th April. . . . The water canoos and yaul made each 1 trip which filled us 2 buts, got off about 1200 lb of rice, but no wood. Will Purcell brought me 3 slaves, 1 man boy, 1 boy (4 foot) and 1 undersize. Tho they are not all such as I should have required of Will Grey had he lived, I think myself pretty well off, and it is indeed the greatest instance of honesty I have met from the blacks at any time to pay me all in such a case. The *Pardoe* weighed at daylight, but to as little purpose as before.

Sunday 28th April. . . . The *Pardoe* still in sight. Quoiled the cables down in the hold and cleared one side of the boys' room for an hospital, having the melancholy appearance of a sickly ship. The canoos made a trip with water, saved a butt and half; 1 load of wood and 2050 lb rice. Settled with one of my traders, Tom Bristol of Black Liverpool town in the river. Loosed the sails but had not time to dry them.

Monday 29th April. . . . The frequent show'rs of rain deter the canoos from making more than one trip. Filled only 1½ butts of water, for have not sent the yaul these 2 days on account of the current which runs stronger in the mornings than she can row ahead. Got one canoo of wood and 650 lb rice. Discharged another trader, John Will of Liverpool Beach town.

Tuesday 30th April. . . . With much ado perswaded the water canoos to make two trips, which with one in the yaul filled us 4 buts. Got off 2 load of wood, and about 900 lb of rice which compleated my purchase. I reckon in the whole I have bought 18,600 lb of which, clear of expence and waste, I have 17,556 lb, which is near 7 tons, 16 cwt in good order in the room. Settled with and discharged all my traders for rice. One more turn of water and wood in the morning will finish this troublesome jobb, for we have only one butt to fill. Considering the season is so far advanced, I think we have had a very favourable opportunity. Lowered the barricado about a foot and new spiked it. Bent the mainsail.

Wednesday 1st May. . . . At 4 a.m. unmored. At 9 the canoos brought the water; discharged them, and at 10 weighed, being then calm but the current setting strong to the offing. At noon the sea brease put in at SW.; we laid just along shoar NW. b W. I think the vessel has found new heels for, tho but an easy brease and she close at it and no appearance of a current to windward, we were abreast of little Cape Mount before sunset. Soon after wind came more up the coast and freshened, continued a fine gale till near midnight, then calmed at same time Cape Mount bore NW. b N., 3 leagues. Passed the French dogger at Little Monserado. Buryed a girl slave (No. 12) of a flux and fever.

Thursday 2nd May. . . . When the sea brease came in, bore away for Mana, being too far southerly to fetch the cape and indifferent to me which place I went first. Anchored at 1 p.m. abreast of the trees in 15 fathoms. Found the Carolina schooner here still waiting for 30 slaves Brian owes him. I had formerly some talk with Mr Smith, one of the managers, about purchasing them of him. Went on board him in the evening and beleive should have come to terms if they had been in his hands. However as Brian is close dunned and been long indebted there is reason to think a few days more will determine it. I therefore proposed to go to Cape Mount, on account of keeping my stock of water, and wait till about Monday, and he engaged (if we agree upon a price) to take every bar's worth of goods off my hands. I offered him 80 bars. He required to trade by invoyce; to allow me 25 per cent upon my sterling prices; and I to take the slaves at £17.10 per head, which will be about 14£ sterling – a dear price upon this coast, but should venture it if I can get no easier, because I have many things on board which will not sell any where and in general poorly assorted.

Fryday 3rd May. . . . At daylight saw a smoke upon the beach, sent the yaul in, returned at 10 with a man that was on board when I was here before, and 2 slaves, a young man and a girl (4 foot 1 inch). Bought them and after dinner put him and the goods ashoar in the yaul. Loosed and aired the sails. Buryed a boy slave (No. 132) of a flux. Have a promise of more trade in the morning if the wind does not suit to sail.

Saturday 4th May. . . . Saw a smoke upon the beach, sent the yaul, brought off a man with 2 slaves, a man and a boy (3 ft 11 inches) bought them and sent the yaul in with the goods. At noon a canoo came on board with a man who calls himself Mr Corker brought 3 good men and a woman girl. I beleive they belong to Mr Bryan, and being indebted to the schooner is ashamed to sell them himself. Bought them and sent the yaul in again in the evening. Have a great deal of trouble in trade by being short of their two principal articles, for I only gave 7 kettles and 21 lb beads upon the 6 slaves.

Sunday 5th May. . . . At 9 a.m. not perceiving any stir upon the beach of more trade, weighed to take the opportunity of getting to Cape Mount, which will hardly offer every day. When we were less than half way, fell calm; at noon the sea brease put in but very faint, that we were till 4 p.m. ere' reached the bay. . . .

Monday 6th May. . . . At sunrise sent the yaul on shoar to Peter Williams to enquire about trade and to ask leave for water. At 10 a canoo came from him with an invitation from him to come on shoar, which was repeated by the yaul when she returned at noon, it being (it seems) beneath his dignity to trade with any one but the master. The yaul brought only 6 casks full, being so much broke she would hardly bear them. At 2 p.m. went on shoar myself to wait on his Majesty. He promised me 5 slaves, but I must go to him again to morrow, they not being then in the town. He is likewise to send a large canoo in the morning for the water casks, for I am willing to spare the boat as much as possible or shall hardly be able to carry her off the coast. In the evening returned on board. The people found 2 knives and a bag of small stones in the men's room.

Tuesday 7th May. . . . At 10 a.m. went on shoar again. Peter Williams showed me 6 slaves out of which I took 5, 2 men, 1 woman, 1 man boy and 1 boy (4 foot). Bought likewise a man from young King Cole, and refused 2 others. In the afternoon came off and paid the goods to George and Peter, Mr Williams' Deputy's. Sent them on shoar in the yaul in the evening. Buryed a man slave (No. 105) of a flux. Made a new awning for the quarter deck of the yaul's sails. Overhalled and reloaded all the arms. A canoo brought us 12 casks of water.

Wednesday 8th May. . . . Came in and anchored the *Africa* from St Pauls. Had George and Peter on board to dinner by invitation. Bought a man slave from the former, and a small boy from a canoo that came from the lowland, likewise a goat. The surf run so high that the canoo could only bring 6 casks of water.

Thursday 9th May. . . . At 7 a.m. went on shoar in the yaul, and Captain Richardson with me, to take leave of the King, or rather to try for some more slaves. Had a very dangerous surf both ways but (thank God) suffered nothing worse than a wetting. Got only my labour for my pains. Brought off 6 of the gang casks empty; the other 6 are at the point full, but to much sea to meddle with them, but he promised to send them off soon in the morning, which is all I wait for. Returned safe on board at 4 p.m. The *Africa's* longboat came in from the Little Cape with 1 slave.

Fryday 10th May. . . . The canoo brought off the casks, but empty, and a small tooth to pay for a spare chain. Attempted to weigh, but when had the anchor just out of the ground, the cable parted. Let go the B.B. as fast as possible, which burst likewise a few minutes afterwards. Were then obliged to make sail and stand off till we bent the end of the sheet cable to the small bower anchor, then tacked in and came too with it in 19 fathoms; but having had a small brease and the current strong, lost about 2 miles. Afterwards sent Mr Marshall in the yaul to borrow Captain Richardson's longboat, but he being on shoar, was obliged to stay till he came off which was near sunsett. Just at dark perceived both boats upon the B.B. buoy, but the great swell hindered their succeeding, being obliged to drop the anchor as soon as they had weighed it. The yaul did not come on board all night. In the evening shifted the small bower and bent the best end to the kedge anchor.

Saturday 11th May. . . . At daylight our yaul purchased the B.B. and brought it on board. At 8 a.m. sent her again for the sheet anchor, which they hooked with a large graplin, and hove about half way up by a spare new rope, then the fluke of the graplin straightened and the anchor run down again, and with the jerk broke the buoy rope. As soon as she returned on board, weighed. At same time a canoo came on board from Mana with a prime man boy and a woman girl. Steered up the coast and at 4 p.m. anchored abreast of Mana trees with the small bower anchor bent to the B.B. cable. Likewise bent the B.B. anchor to the sheet cable. Bought the slaves and the trader promises another in the morning. . . .

Sunday 12th May. . . . In the forenoon hove up the anchor to look at; being clear, let it go again. Bought a man and a girl (4 feet 1 inch) from a quiet fellow who called himself Jemmy, which took away my last kettle, except 1 broke, and the remainder of my beads, so that I beleive my trade for this voyage is finished. However, shall wait here till morning because the man that was on board yesterday promised to sell me 2 more for arms and powder. Buryed a man slave (No. 101) of a fever. Saved a french butt of rain water.

Monday 13th May. . . . At 9 a.m., no canoo offering to come off, weighed. . . . The sea brease came in so far up the coast that I was afraid we should not weather the Gallina's point. At 3 p.m. came too about 1 league short of it in 14 fathoms with the best anchor, it blowing strong and a very high sea. The Carolina schooner at anchor 2 miles to windward. Sent the yaul to let Mr Smith know that I was now ready to trade with him upon his former terms, but he has no slaves yet. All night bad weather; filled 6 gang casks with rain water. Passed us in the offing the *Brittannia* schooner, Thurston.

Tuesday 14th May. . . . Weighed at 3 a.m. with the first of the land wind. Steered along the shoar NW., at noon fell calm and soon after had the sea brease at WSW. Having a good offing, made a long slant, and at 8 p.m. came too in 12 fathoms, I reckon about 7 or 8 leagues below Shebar. Filled a butt of rain water.

Wednesday 15th May. . . . Made the best of it we could all day and at dark anchored in 12 fathoms, the high trees of Shebar NW. b N. 3 leagues. Towards midnight wind came off the land with rain. Filled 5 gang casks of water. A high swell makes the vessel labour very much. At work all spare times mending the sails, yet cannot repair them half so fast as the rats destroy. We have so many on board that they are ready to devour every thing, and actually bite the people when they catch them asleep, and have even begun to nibble at the cables.

Thursday 16th May. . . . At 11 a.m. came too with the B.B. at Shebar in 14 fathoms water, soft ground, the high trees N. b W., not chusing to run too far in lest I find difficulty of clearing the bar, if I should want to sail before a good land wind offers. Afterwards sent the yaul to the beach; she returned at sunsett and informed me that Mr Tucker attempted to come off with a good parcel of slaves, but the canoo was stove in the surf at first launching. The sea brease tumbled in an exceeding high swell in the afternoon, as is customary about full and change; makes us ride very hard and broke one of the larboard main shrouds, the first peice of rigging I remember to have given way the voyage.

Fryday 17th May. Squally weather, wind about SW. and a great sea. The ship labours prodigiously, broke the main topmast stay. At daylight sent the yaul to the beach; she returned about noon, brought 7 men slaves from Mr Tucker. He would willingly come off himself but the surf run very high, and sunk the canoo loaded with camwood. Filled more than a but of rain water. Buryed a man slave (No. 34) of a flux and fever. Boatswain at work securing the main rigging.

> ['For about seven months in this country the weather is remarkably fair, with light winds, and seldom a threatening cloud to be seen. In the remaining five, we have either incessant heavy rains, or sudden storms of wind, with violent thunder and rain. This uncomfortable season is now commencing. Two hundred people confined in a small vessel, in bad weather, occasion noise, dirt, and trouble enough.'—From *Letters to a Wife*.]

Saturday 18th May. . . . Sent the yaul to the beach; Mr Tucker came off in her to dinner and staid on board all night. Brought with him a man boy, a girl (4 feet) a girl (3 ft 10 ins) and a small boy. Have had a very strong windward current all day, and a great southern swell makes us roul and labour very much. Received 6 cwt of camwood for ½ a ton, the rest lost in the surf.

Sunday 19th May. . . . Sent the yaul on shoar with Mr Tucker, and in the afternoon his shallop and canoo came from over the bar. Put in them the remainder of our arms, pewter, brass, etc., and some other things that would be spoiled if carried off the coast, with 60 iron bars and some powder to make them passable, for which he gave me his note of hand when on board, to pay next voyage. They left a few things to be sent by the yaul in the morning. From sunset till midnight very coarse weather, hard rain, strong gusts of wind from the sea, and a very high swell, violent thunder and lightning and several meteors flying about the rigging. . . .

Monday 20th May. . . . Sent Mr Marshall in the yaul with the rest of the goods and to sign receipts for some more slaves I expected from Mr Tucker. They stove 2 canoos in the surf attempting to come off to him, and he was at last obliged to swim on shoar, and the boat, after waiting till night, came off without him. I hear Joseph Tucker is come down with his 2 slaves; they attempted to come over the bar in a shallop, but were constrained to go back, the unsettled weather yesterday having caused a violent sea upon the bar and beach too. Got up the top gallant yards. In the night 2 slaves that have been long ill of a flux dyed. A man (No. 113) and a girl (No. 129).

Tuesday 21st May. . . . In the morning saw the shallop coming over the bar; at 1 p.m. she came on board with Mr Marshall, Joseph Tucker and a man and woman girl, slaves he owed me, and payed so promptly in expectation of having more goods till next voyage as he called it; but dismissed without anything. Sent the yaul with provisions to the people in Mr T.'s longboat who have been fasting since Sunday noon, and can neither get over the bar, nor is any canoo upon the beach to come off to assist them. Afterwards got all ready for sailing but had no slant of wind any way. Buryed a fine woman girl of a fever which destroyed her in 5 days. The doctor was taken ill yesterday and is now worse with a fever and vomiting.

Wednesday 22nd May. . . . At 3 a.m. weighed with a small brease at West, bound (by God's permission) for Antigua. Stood off from South to SW. b S. as the wind allowed, sat all sails. Made but little way by reason of the great head swell and the brease faint, but just at noon freshened a little; at same time the high trees of Shebar bear North. . . . Saw the Carolina schooner at anchor under the land, beleive Mr Smith was coming to trade with me. He said he would if he got any slaves, but as I limited him to 4 days he can't well blame me, it being 9 since I was with him.

Thursday 23rd May. . . . Buryed a man slave (No. 34). . . . I take my departure from Shebar, which by my own observation lyes in Lattitude 7° 20^{m}. I am obliged to estimate the longitude myself for it is not laid down in the books, and those places that are, very incorrectly—Cape Mount in the *Mariner's Compass* being supposed in nearly the same meridian with Sierra Leon in the *Kalendar*, tho there are more than 2° difference. I have good reasons and authority to determine the longitude of Sierra Leon at about 13° 10^{m} from London, and I reckon Shebar is 50^{m} more easterly, that is 12° 20^{m}.

Fryday 24th May. Fair pleasant weather, light airs and calms . . . and smooth water. Sounded several times for fear that I should have been unexpectedly drawn too near the Shoals of St Anne. At midnight tacked, afterwards had seldom wind sufficient to give the ship steeridge way, for she is now so foul she will not feel a small brease. Aired some of the spare sails.

['I have lost sight of Africa, . . . innumerable dangers and difficulties, which, without a superior protection, no man could escape or surmount, are, by the goodness of God, happily over. . . . It is now ten in the evening. I am going to walk the deck and think of you; and, according to my constant custom, to recommend you to the care and protection of God.' From *Letters to a Wife*.]

Saturday 25th May. . . . Tacked several times for the advantage of the breases. At 10 p.m. took in small sails; sounded, as likewise at 12 and afterwards every half hour. At 3 a.m. got ground at 30 fathoms off the edge of St Ann's shoal, and at daylight could see the islands off Cape St Anne's. . . .

Sunday 26th May. . . . In the evening, by the favour of Providence, discovered a conspiracy among the men slaves to rise upon us, but a few hours before it was to have been executed. A young man, No. —, who has been the whole voyage out of irons, first on account of a large ulcer, and since for his seeming good behaviour, gave them a large marline spike down the gratings, but was happily seen by one of the people. They had it in possesion about an hour before I mad search for it, in which time they made such good dispatch (being an instrument that made no noise) that this morning I've found near 20 of them had broke their irons. Are at work securing them.

Monday 27th May. . . . A hard tornado came on so quick that had hardly time to take in a small sail; blew extream hard for 3 hours with heavy rain. . . . At noon little wind. . . . In the afternoon secured all the men's irons again and punished 6 of the ringleaders of the insurrection. To agree with my observation I allow the course made good as steered, tho there is 8° or 9° variation, the difference I beleive owing to a northerly current, for I have perceived a strange ripling all the morning.

Tuesday 28th May. . . . Secured the after bulkhead of the men's room, for they had started almost every stantient. Their plot was excedingly well laid, and had they been let alone an hour longer, must have occasioned us a good deal of trouble and damage. I have reason to be thankfull they did not make attempts upon the coast when we had often 7 or 8 of our best men out of the ship at a time and the rest busy. They still look very gloomy and sullen and have doubtless mischeif in their heads if they could find opportunity to vent it. But I hope (by the Divine Assistance) we are fully able to overawe them now. . . .

Wednesday 29th May. . . . At noon a tornado from the eastward . . . hard rain; filled 4 casks of water. Brought some camwood and the 4 guns from forward to aft, the ship being too much by the head. . . . Buryed a boy slave (No. 86) of a flux. Had 3 girls taken with fevers this morning. . . . The moon was eclipsed about ¾ths. Began to be dark at ½ past 10 and continued till 40 minutes past one by our glass, but beleive it was far enough from exact.

* * *

Saturday 1st June. . . . In the night broke a main shroud. At midnight, 4 a.m. and noon sounded for fear of the shoals of Rio Grande; could get no ground with 70 fathoms. By my reckoning should be 30 leagues without them, and by the number of dolphins about us, and not seeing any sunfish, which are generally very plenty about the banks, I hope I cannot be much nearer, but am something uneasy as it might be of the last ill consequence to be catched upon them at this season.

* * *

Fryday 7th June. . . . At 9 a.m. departed this life Gideon Measham, who came ill out of the longboat, the 28th March, of a fever which he recovered from, but has been otherwise declining ever since. . . .

* * *

Monday 10th June. Cloudy weather and very cold for the climate, for which reason have not had the slaves upon deck these 2 days, and can hardly keep them warm in the rooms. . . .

Tuesday 11th June. . . . Close dark weather and incredibly cold, considering we have the sun almost in the zenith. I think I have felt it (sensibly) much warmer in England at Michaelmass. Am obliged to keep the slaves close down, and even the tarpawlins laid over. Began yesterday to shave them all and this morning finished. Hands at work mending the sails we unbent lately.

Wednesday 12th June. . . . Got the slaves up this morn. Washed them all with fresh water. They complained so much of cold that was obliged to let them go down again when the rooms were cleaned. Buryed a man slave (No. 84) of a flux, which he has been strugling with near 7 weeks. . . .

Thursday 13th June. . . . This morning buryed a women slave (No. 47). Know not what to say she died of for she has not been properly alive since she first came on board.

* * *

Sunday 16th June. In the afternoon we were alarmed with a report that some of the men slaves had found means to poyson the water in the scuttle casks upon deck, but upon enquiry found they had only conveyed some of their country fetishes, as they call them, or talismans into one of them, which they had the credulity to suppose must inevitably kill all who drank of it. But if it please God thay make no worse attempts than to charm us to death, they will not much harm us, but it shews their intentions are not wanting. . . .

* * *

Tuesday 18th June. . . . The air is so sharp that the slaves cannot stand the deck, not even to mess or wash. In the forenoon passed a few small parcels of gulphweed.

* * *

Thursday 20th June. . . . This morning buryed 2 slaves, a man (No. 140) of a flux, and a boy (No. 170) of the gravel and stoppage of urine. Washed the slaves with fresh water. Picked out 4 of our best helmsmen as temoneers to steer the ship down the parallel.

* * *

Saturday 22nd June.... Carpenter finished the yaul; she is now in almost as good order as when we first had her. In the fore noon, being pretty warm, got up the men and washed all the slaves with fresh water. I am much afraid of another ravage from the flux, for we have had 8 taken within these few days. Have seen 2 or 3 tropick birds and a few flying fish.

Saturday [*Sunday*] *23rd June....* Have a few more flying fish about us, but no birds or gulphweed yet. The longitude of Antigua by Dr Halley's chart and the Table in the *Mariner's Compass* is 60° 30^{m} from London. I am therefore this day at noon, by my reckoning, 132 leagues distant from it, provided my computation of the longitude of Sierra Leon is right.

Monday 24th June.... Buryed a boy slave (No. 158) of a flux.... Obliged to condemn the best bower [cable] as far in as the splice. Have seen 1 gull and 1 booby, but few flying fish and no gulph weed. Distance *ab* Antigua, 95 leagues.

Tuesday 25th June.... Do not yet perceive any indications of drawing near the land, only we have a few more flying fish about us, but no others. Distance *ab* Antigua, 64 leagues....

Wednesday 26th June.... Turned the yaul and coated her with pitch tar and brimstone.... Saw several small parcells of gulphweed and 2 men of war birds, few or no flying fish. Distance *ab* Antigua, 36 leagues.

Thursday 27th June.... By my reckoning I should be only 8 leagues distance from Antigua, but I must be mistaken or I should see it, for the weather is indifferent clear.

Fryday 28th June.... Buryed a girl slave (No. 172) of a flux.

Saturday 29th June.... Have seen several men of war, boobies and other fowls and frequent flocks of small birds. Have likewise a good many flying fish about us, but no gulphweed. No appearance of land. Buryed a man slave (No. 2) of a flux he has sustained about 3 months. Washed the slaves with fresh water.

Sunday 30th June.... Saw 2 sloops standing to the southward. Run under an easy sail all night, at daylight saw a brig to the northward steering our way. Halled up and spoke her. She is from New Providence bound for St Christophers. The master reckoned himself then 13 leagues to the eastward of Antigua.

Monday 1st July.... The brig a league to the NW. At 10 a.m. saw a sloop to the NE., standing to the southward. Buryed a man slave (No. 36) of a flux. I begin to think long for the land, for I did not expect to find so large an error in my reckoning.

Tuesday 2nd July. Very squally troublesome weather.... At daylight saw the land and to my no small surprize found it to be Berbuda [Barbuda], bearing from the SSW. to the WNW, 3 leagues. A sloop from Bermuda's whom we spoke over night in company with us, halled close off....

Wednesday 3rd July.... At 4 p.m. perceived the sloop standing off, being to leeward of us, as we happened to be laid better for the veering of the breases; when she was pretty near, tacked and stood in before us. At dark were about the middle of the island, it bearing SW. b S. 3 leagues, we lying up SSE. At midnight tacked off, being as near as I durst venture by the light of the moon in such a foul island, but the sloop carried it round. At 3 a.m. we tacked to the southward again, and the wind favoured us just enough to weather every thing, and I beleive not a mile to spare. Were abreast of the southernmost breakers at 9 a.m., and soon after saw Antigua; bore away for it.... At 2 p.m. the pilot came on board we being about 2 leagues without the reaf . . . afterwards plyed till sunset, when came too with the small bower in St Johns Road, the harbour open and 5 fathoms water.

The next page of the Journal is blank and the next entry is dated 13th August, when the ship began the homeward voyage to Liverpool. At Antigua, Newton received a letter informing him that his father, who had been appointed Governor of Fort York in Hudson's Bay, had been drowned while bathing.

On 20th July Newton wrote a long letter to the Rev. David Jennings, D.D., in which he observed: 'Putting the other world out of the question, it seems necessary to be a Christian in order to preserve any tolerable degree of peace amidst the fluctuating inconstant scenes of this. If any unprejudiced person would compare Horace, Lib 1, Ode 22, and Lib 3, Ode 4, with the 46th and 90th Psalms, or the contradictory doubtfull consolations of Cicero with St Luke 12th, Vs. 4 and 8, and many similar passages in the New Testament, I think this argument alone must be convincing....'

With another letter, undated, to Dr Jennings, Newton sends 'a quarto book of occasional thoughts which I filled the last voyage by way of exercise on Sundays according to the advice of Mr. Bennet and, as far as I was able . . . in so confused a scene as a slaving ship . . . the example of Sir Matthew Hale'. Presumably Newton had read, *The Life and Death of Sir Matthew Hale*, by Burnet (London, 1682).

On 23rd July he wrote to his wife referring to the music of Handel and to Garrick playing *Hamlet*; and on 4th August (a Sunday) he wrote: 'You will perceive by the date that this is one of the days which I pass, as much as I can, in retirement and reflection.']

Tuesday 13th August.... At 9 this morning began to unmoor, and at 11 weighed in St John's Harbour, bound (by God's permission) for Liverpool.

At noon are abreast of the Wellington rock; hoisted in the yaul and discharged the pilot. The ship very full and lumbered....

Wednesday 14th August.... At 6 p.m. the West end of Antigua bore SSE. 8 leagues, from whence take my Departure. Were very busy the afternoon cleaning decks. Stowed the anchor upon the forecastle, unbent the cables, and with a good deal of trouble quoiled them down below. Saw a ship to the eastward steering our way, suppose she is the *Blizard*, Hawkin, for London, who was to sail from Parham on Monday night.

['I am sitting by a person in his last agonies, and who, only five days since, was healthy and florid. This is my surgeon, who, by an obliging behaviour during the whole voyage, has gained a great share of my regard. But I fear he must go.... *From Letters to a Wife*.]

* * *

Saturday 17th August.... At 6 a.m. departed this life Mr Robert Arthur, our surgeon, of a fever which seized him a few days before we left St John's. I would willingly have persuaded him to stay behind, but could not, as he did not apprehend himself in so much danger (nor indeed any one else) as he really was.

Sunday 18th August. The former part very hard gales ... and a lofty sea, the latter moderate. At 2 p.m. came on a most violent squall which I was much afraid was the beginning of a hurricane, for I do not remember to have met any thing equal to it since I have used the sea. It laid the sea for a time in a manner smooth, but the spoon drift flew so thick that could hardly see the length of a ship. We had not time to take in the mainsail which to my great surprize sustained it without damage. It pleased God it lasted hardly an hour, and afterward the weather began to break up....

* * *

Fryday 23rd August.... Have seen a ship all this forenoon about 3 leags. to windward standing our way, I suppose it may be the *Blizard*, but is too far off to distinguish any particulars.

Saturday 24th August. ... In the afternoon lost sight of the sail, but at daylight saw her again to the NE. by N. about the same distance as yesterday and I think we gain upon her....

Sunday 25th August. ... The ship about 2 leagues to the northward. Shewed either or french or St George's colours; cannot be certain which it was as it was calm. See a snow to the southward likewise bound our way.

Monday 26th August.... The ship about 3 leagues to the northward and the snow a league to the SE. I take her to be a townsman, but cannot induce her to show an ensign. This morning tarred the sides.

Tuesday 27th August. . . . Spoke the snow, proved a Frenchman from Martinico for Louisburg. . . .

* * *

Monday 9th September. For the most part a very hard gale . . . with a high following sea; hazey weather and some squalls of rain.

> ['I am in good health, I am surrounded by a good Providence, to which a calm and a storm are alike; and, as the wind is fair, every puff pushes me nearer to you. I have shortened the distance between us about one hundred and eighty miles within the last twenty-four hours.' From *Letters to a Wife*.]

* * *

Monday 16th September. The first part rainy weather and hard gales, the latter foggy and moderate; a jumbling swell from several quarters. In the afternoon passed a snow steering to the westward. At noon beginning to blow again.

> ['The scene is much changed since yesterday. The wind is abated, and the raging billows are greatly subsided. I thank God we did not sustain the least damage, though such seasons are not without real danger; for the force of the sea when enraged by the wind, is inconceivable by those who have not seen it, and unmanageable by those who have seen the most of it.' From *Letters to a Wife*.]

Tuesday 17th September. Dank foggy weather, light gales as per log and smooth water. At 6 a.m. after an hour's calm a fine brease sprung up westerly, which cleared the air something. At 8 saw a snow very near us standing to the northward, showed our Jack which she returned and soon after tacked to the southward. At noon have lost sight of her. By observation to day I was in Lattitude 44° 13^{m}, but the horizon was so thick and uncertain, that I do not chuse to depend upon it so far as to correct my reckoning.

* * *

Thursday 19th September. . . . A strong gale and squally with a high northern sea, afterwards moderate; fine clear weather, water smooth and more westerly.

> [A long letter expounding one of Aesop's fables, ending: 'I know not what I should digress to next, but I am just told, the tea kettle boils; so, as the sailors say, no more at present.' From *Letters to a Wife*.]

Fryday 20th September. . . . A strong gale with a very high western sea. Broke a main shroud on the starboard side. . . .

['Another heavy gale and it is not easy to sit fast, or to hold a pen . . . the distance between us is lessening at the rate of seven or eight miles per hour. Imagine to yourself an immense body of water behind you, higher than a house, and a chasm of equal depth just before you . . . in the twinkling of an eye the ship descends into the pit which is gasping to receive her, and with equal swiftness ascends to the top on the other side before the mountain that is behind can overtake her. And this is repeated as often as you can deliberately count four.' From *Letters to a Wife.*]

Saturday 21st September. Till midnight had a hard gale . . . and a wild sky, afterwards moderate and towards daylight proved exceeding fine pleasant weather. At 1 p.m. took the 2nd reaf in the F.T.S., at 3 handed it, the sea running deep and dangerous. . . .

Sunday 22nd September. . . . Saw a ship steering about ESE. At 10 a.m. the wind flew out to the southward with rain and blows fresh at noon.

Monday 23rd September. . . . At noon is clear sharp weather and a strong gale, a great WNW. sea, but we go incomparably easy and dry thro it, hardly shipping a single spray.

* * *

Fryday 27th September. . . . Sounded, no ground at 80 fathoms, neither did I expect to find any according to my reckoning, but chuse to be certain. . . . Have a great many gulls and sheerwater about us, and this morning saw a butterfly.

* * *

Monday 30th September. . . . A sail to the NW. (a brig) standing our way and seems to head reach us fast.

Tuesday 1st October. At 1 p.m. bore down and spoke to the brig, being of and for Bristol from Newfoundland, only 12 days out. The master reckoned himself 75 leagues to the westward of Cape Clear. . . . By my reckoning I am, at noon, 19 leagues to the westward of Cape Clear.

Wednesday 2nd October. . . . As I have overun my difference in longitude I must depend upon a good look out instead of a bad reckoning. This morning the people, going down into the fore peek to get fire wood, perceived a constant small ofrun of water coming over the hooks, and upon examination we found that it had entirely washed the sugar out of a teirce that is stowed on the starboard side of the foremast, and I am afraid has done more damage, tho I can see no fault in the stowage. We have kept one pump jogging for the most part since we left Antigua, which is so customary with deep loaden ships after having been long light upon the coast, that I had no suspicion of her making water – only in her upper works. We cannot come at it to do any good.

Thursday 3rd October. . . . I have already exceeded the Bristolman's reckoning about 5 leagues, so he is mistaken as well as me, tho not so much, and as he had a very short passage, I am in hopes he was not greatly out, but cannot perceive the least signs of approaching the land as yet. . . .

Fryday 4th October. . . . At 6 p.m. took a reaf in each top sail; at the same time sounded, no ground at 90 fathoms up and down. At 8 a.m. sounded again, struck ground at about 65 fathoms, very coarse brown sand with small stones and peices of shells. Halled up . . . and just at noon saw the land bearing NNE. about 7 leagues distant, but it is so hazey cannot yet know it. No good observation.

Saturday 5th October. At 3 p.m. were within a league of the land, but it was so extream thick we could not know it certainly. I took it for Castle Haven, steered along shoar East. At 8 p.m. made the light upon the old head of Kinsale. . . . But as I could not be assured it might not be Waterford, halled off . . . to avoid the Saltees. Afterwards had very fine, clear weather. At daylight perceived my caution was needless, for we were only abreast of Cork and about 7 leagues from the land. At noon Bally-cotton Island bears North 4 leagues. Have seen a ship and a snow, both plyers. Got the anchors over the bows.

Sunday 6th October. . . . Exceeding fair pleasant weather. . . . At 5 p.m. Dungarvon head bore N. b W., distance 4 leagues. At 9 saw Waterford light, were up with it at 11, about 5 leagues distant. At 4 reckoning myself past the Saltees, halled in for the channel. At noon the land of Arklow bears WNW. distance 6 leagues.

Monday 7th October. . . . At 6 p.m. the Hill of Hoath bore N. b W. 7 leagues. . . . Made Holy head to the SE. at midnight. . . . Found a strong ebb and a very great sea. At 4 a.m. perceived the tide to be changed in our favour. At 5 the Skirries [Skerries] SW. 3 leagues. At 8 past Beaumaris, and at noon the Great Ormshead SSW. 2 leagues. . . . In company with the Liverpool merchant from Mary-land.

Till midnight fair weather and winds variable. . . . At 4 p.m. got a pilot on board, worked up the flood to hyle-lake [Hoylake], and anchored at 10 just within the buoy.

Soli Deo Gloria

The Second Voyage

30TH JUNE 1752 – 29TH AUGUST 1753

[About the 25th October 1751 Newton was free from his duties in Liverpool and went to Chatham. Early in April 1752 he returned to Liverpool and saw his new ship, the *African,* in Fisher's yard upon the stocks. Fourteen months later he described the *African* as 'one of the strongest vessels that can be built for money . . . but she is a very indifferent sailor'. On 19th April he wrote in his Diary: 'Upon the launching the new Vessel yesterday on which my next voyage to Africa is designed: I thought the occasion contrary to the usual custom of festivity and extravagance, rather called for a very serious frame and I determined to take the first convenient opportunity of being alone to recommend the event of this undertaking to my Gracious God.'

On 3rd June he wrote to Dr Jennings: '. . . I would willingly interest the prayers of all good people in my behalf and prepose to put up bills on all publick places of worship in this town on Sunday next and as it is the custom here to mention every body by name I shall be glad of an opportunity of telling so many thousand people at once, that tho' I shall be at least equal in all external advantages, with any ship that goes abroad, yet I depend only and entirely upon the blessing of the Almighty for success in any degree . . . the latter part of my life has been generally very smooth, and I have not been so much supported under a series of real dangers and difficulties, as preserved even from the smallest appearance of them. . . . I expect to sail if opportunity offers in ten days. . . .'

On 5th July 1752, he wrote in his Diary: 'At sea. This day I have reason to be particularly observant of my Duty in keeping the Sabbath holy to the Lord both as it is the first opportunity I have had of convening my ship's company to beg a publick blessing from Almighty God upon our voyage; and farther as it is a day appointed . . . for celebrating the sacrament of the body and blood of my Lord Jesus, in which communion tho' I cannot personally join yet my heart and thoughts ought to be engaged upon so interesting a theme.'

He resolved never to sleep longer than 7 hours, perhaps 6. 'I would look upon it as in a manner criminal to exceed 8 at any time. . . .' He intended to begin every morning with one hour in prayer and reading the Bible, 'or if not otherwise hindered 2 hours'. After that, 'I may safely go on with my purpose of improving myself in the Latin and french languages and the mathematicks, recreating my mind and unbending it'. When he had much leisure time he would 'find another opportunity of solemn prayer and devotion' at midday. In his prayers he would remember relations, friends, benefactors, enemies ('if I have any') and 'more generally the race of mankind'. Amongst other things he would pray for Christian unity, for the spirit of grace and amendment 'upon all debauched and profane persons such as I myself too long was', and that 'by a constant chearfulness' he might show his ship's company that the ways of religion and true wisdom are ways of pleasantness. Every Sunday he would have public prayers morning and evening. The next page of the Journal lists the ship's company.]

Officers and Seamen belonging to the *African*, 1752. 1753
(*Commenced pay* 1752 *June* 30th)

Names	*Quality*
John Newton	Master
Alexander Welsh	first Mate
Thomas Henbury	Surgeon
James Billinge	second Mate
David Webster	Carpenter
James Boyd	Boatswain
Theophilus Strickland	Cooper, run 17th June 1753
Joseph Fellowes	Steward. Discharged 23rd August to go in the *Thistle,* Bray of Bristol. [Shipped as second Mate.]
James White	Cook
James Tootal	Carpenter's Mate. Run 1st July 1753
Jacob Robinson	Fore the mast
Edward Eaton	do.
Joseph Forrester	do. Discharged 14th December }
Richard Swain	do. Discharged 14th December }
	[Sent by the *Earl of Hallifax,* Thomson of London, to be put on board the first man of war for misdemeanour.]
Joseph White	Gunner[1]
James Wilkinson	Fore the mast. Run 4th October
Thomas Harrington	do.
William Cunneigh	do.
Richard Griffith	do.
Peter Mackdonald	Ordinary. Deceased 19th November
John Sadler	do. Run 1st July 1753
James Morgan	Ship's Apprentice
Robert Cropper	do.
James Leland	do.
Jonathan Ireland	do.
Edmund Whitaker	do.
21st November	
Thomas Gibson	F mast. Discharged 13th June per agreement

[1] 'To take care of the small arms and act as gunner; upon his good behaviour he is to have 2/6 per month, extra wages.'—*Journal*, 4th August 1752.

Laus Deo

Journal of a voyage intended (by God's permission) in the African, *snow, from Liverpool to the windward coast of Africa, etc., 1752.*

Tuesday 30th June. At daylight this morning unmored, and at 11, being high water, weighed from the Black Rock, in company with the *Adlington*, John Perkins, for windward and Gold Coast....

* * *

Thursday 9th July.... Thermometer at 60° Farenhaits. Scale at noon. Freezing point at 32°.[2]

* * *

Wednesday 12th August.... At 9 saw the looming of the land, and at 10 breakers ... soon after, clearing up, perceived we had Cape Sierra Leon eastward about 3 miles and that the breakers were upon the rock....

Thursday 13th August.... In the morning King Peter of Whiteman's bay sent for his duty, but having heard yesterday that he had been very lately deposed, I put them off till the morrow, and at noon an embassy arrived from his new majesty Seignor Don Pedro de Case upon the same errand, with a written testimonial from Seignor Don de Lopez, the undoubted king-maker of Sierra Leon. Upon consideration I found reason to recognize his title preferably to the former, and paid his demand of 16 bars, which, by the bye, is 4 more than was required by any of his predecessors; but with new kings there will be new laws. I have the honour to be second upon his list....

Fryday 14th August.... King Peter sent a man to forbid me fetching wood or water from his port....

Saturday 15th August.... King Peter came on board, having altered his mind and gave me liberty for wood and water; brought a fine man slave with him, but had not time to pay for him, being busy with Mr Steele who came in last night from Kissy Kissy, bought 4 men slaves off him. I find the price is established at 70 bars amongst the whites....

Sunday 16th August.... Paid King Peter for his man and lent him goods for 3 slaves, likewise made him a present in lieu of his former duty which had a good effect, for in the afternoon he brought off 2 very good boys....

Monday 17th August.... At daylight went to the King's town. He shewed me 2 fine men, which I brought on board with me. Refused a woman....

[2] Newton's first reference to the use of a thermometer. From this date he recorded the temperature daily.

Tuesday 18th August. . . . Went on shoar to the King's town and got a boy slave. . . . Bought likewise about half an ounce of gold. . . .

Wednesday 19th August. . . . Sent the King a cag of brandy, being a court day with him. . . .

Thursday 20th August. . . . Had a visit from Seignor Peter Case, the new king. Got 2 small servilas from the other king. . . .

Fryday 21st August. . . . Peter Case made another visit, brought with him a man from whom I bought a man boy, half a ton of cam wood in 48 peices, 2 teeth (weight 43 lb) and a cwt of rice.

* * *

Monday 24th August. . . . A canoo from the Bullan Shore brought 4 prime slaves on board. When I was paying for them they took an exception to the smallness of the powder cags, and insisted upon having them half a bar under price. I was determined not to shew so ill a precedent, and so with a good deal of regret I suffered them to take them on shoar again. They have not yet carryed them on board any other vessel. . . .

Tuesday 25th August. . . . Thermometer at 78 where it lyes in the desk, but when I placed it in the heat of the sun at noon it rose to 100: I was surprized to find so great a difference.

* * *

Wednesday 2nd September. . . . Came in a shallop of Mr Langton's from Cissy with 6 slaves but are all consigned to the *Hunter*.

Thursday 14th September. . . . Have altered the stile to day in obedience to the act of Parliament. [The Act adopting the New Style or Gregorian calendar.]

Fryday 15th September. . . . At 8 a.m. the *Hunter* weighed to go up to the factory. I went up in her, partly to talk with the gentlemen there, and partly to acquaint myself with the channel, as I propose to clean the ship there some months hence [see 25th March 1753] and pilots are scarce and intolerable dear. . . . I find the marks are very plain, and but little difficulty or risque in the navigation. I beleive I need expect no trade from this quarter, as they expect to be regularly supplied with vessels of their own.

* * *

Saturday 23rd September. . . . Had the Captain of the *Badger* with his purser and surgeon on board to dinner. Saluted him twice with 7 guns. [3]

Sunday 24th September. . . . I have refused 7 slaves yesterday and today, being either lame, old or blind. The frenchmen [commanded by M. Gervaizeau] drives a great trade, and it is reported has bought near 40

[3] H.M.S. *Badger*, a sloop, Captain John Hale.

since he came in, but I beleive many if not most are of some of the above qualities. . . .

* * *

Thursday 5th October. . . . Between 1 and 2 a.m., the watch upon deck being either asleep or consenting, 2 of the people, viz. James Wilkinson and Richard Griffith run away with the yaul, tho chained, but I suppose they unreaved the chain when sent to lock it in the evening. At daylight perceived her lying at the watering place, borrowed a boat and luckily brought her off before the blacks knew she had been in their power, otherwise she would have cost me, I suppose, at least 60 bars; then sent to the King to offer a reward for apprehending my people. . . .

* * *

Fryday 20th October. . . . [*At Shebar*.] Went in shoar myself in the yaul. A canoo came off for me and brought 5 slaves from Mr Tucker. Landed safe about 11 not without some difficulty and a thorough wetting. Sent the yaul on board.

On Monday sent the yaul to fill water. Came safe over the bar but know not when she will get out; tryed 3 days running while I was on shoar but in vain. On Wednesday I saw the longboat was returned. On Thursday endeavoured to get off in a canoo, but after being twice filled, was obliged to desist. On Fryday morning attempted again; I, being very much out of order, got safe on board about noon, and found everything well (*Deo gratias*).

[There are no entries in the Journal between 21st and 28th October inclusive. On the 31st Newton wrote to his wife: 'Since my last I have been a week on shore, and three or four days indisposed.']

Sunday 29th October. . . . Nothing remarkable except that the bar should be impassable for so many days together in the dry season and the moon near the quarters. . . .

* * *

Thursday 2nd November. . . . Begun to day with arms and centinels . . .

[To guard the slaves, there being now about 20 men slaves on board.]

* * *

Friday 10th November.

['I have been walking the deck very pleasantly. It is my watch, for the ship is under sail. These silent night hours, when the weather is fair, are, to me, the most agreable part of the voyage: for in the day-time, the heat of the sun, the smoke of the furnace, and the hurry of trade, are a little troublesome; I mean they would be so, did not the thoughts of you interpose to enliven the scene. But when the sun is set, the fires out, and all but the watch are asleep, I can enjoy myself without disturbance.'—From *Letters to a Wife.*]

Saturday 11th November. [*At sea between Shebar and Mana.*] . . . At 7 a.m. weighed, but the wind soon after flew out to the southward, came too again. Had afterwards excessive rain for 2 hours with violent thunder and lightning. One clap in particular broke (seemingly) quite on board us, and a sort of fire ball went over the vessel amidships, very near the deck, but, thank God, no damage ensued. Two of the people felt a shock, and one of them could not use his arm for an hour or two afterwards. . . .

* * *

Tuesday 14th November. [*At Mana.*] At daylight perceived the longboat in the offing. At 8 a.m. she came on board, brought with her the *Mercy Gee*'s punt with 4 hands and the doctor, their vessel having left them at the Gallina's. We are informed by them that the ship we saw here was the *Ellis and Robert,* Jackson; that the *Addlington* is down at or about Bassa with near 200 slaves on board, and that there [has] been an insurrection in her, in which the cheif mate and 19 slaves were killed. The longboat brought a letter and 4 men slaves from Mr Clow, and left goods with him for about 4 more. Had a canoo from the shoar with 4 slaves, refused them all, 2 being too old, and 2 too young. Lent Jemmy Cole goods for 4 slaves. Sent the yaul in shoar with them and some of Mr Tucker's people, and she did not come on board all night. Have the boatswain and 3 more people ill of a fever.

Wednesday 15th November. . . . The yaul returned at 9 a.m. . . . Her long stay, making me very uneasy, gave occasion to the discovering a plot some of our people had been concerned in, which I can suppose to be no less than seizing the ship. William Coney, the informer, told me he had been solicited by Richard Swain to sign what he called a round robin, a term which I was before stranger to. I cannot but acknowledge a visible interposition of Divine Providence, for tho I cannot yet find the bottom of it, I have reason to think this sickness we have had on board within these 3 days has prevented a black design when it was almost ripe for execution, and the unexpected stay of the boat brought it to light. I thought myself very secure from any danger of this kind, as every body has behaved very quiet the whole voyage and I do not remember the least complaint or grievance. Richard Swain was then in the yaul; as soon as she came on board I put him in double irons. He seemed to be much surprized and pretends he knows nothing of the matter. The others [of] whom I have suspicion are at present too ill to bear examining. . . .

Thursday 16th November. . . . I hope the boatswain and one of our sick are in a fair way of recovery, for we are at present so weak that can do nothing when the yaul is away, but be upon our guard against the slaves and the round robin gentlemen; and what makes it more difficult, I am not yet able to find out who are or are not in the gang. . . .

Fryday 17th November. . . . In the evening made some farther discovery concerning the round-robins. Joseph Forrester and Peter Mackdonald were it seems parties, and were providentially both taken sick in one day; the latter is so ill I hardly expect he can live, but the former I think recovered enough to be put in irons. My second witness is John Sadler, who says, when he was in the boat at Shebar he heard Swain and Forrester talk to each other, but in a distant manner, that he could not understand then what he intended; the one said somebody should pay for it, and the other that he was sure all the ship's company would join him if he spoke the word. But at another time he heard Joseph Forrester in plain terms say that he would kill Mr Welsh and the doctor, or at least leave only just alive. He likewise says that when the yaul was on shoar on Wednesday, Swain endeavoured to perswade him and the rest to go off with her.

Saturday 18th November. At daylight put Joseph Forrester in irons, then sent the yaul to the beach. She returned at noon with an invitation from Mr Brian to come on shoar, which I complyed with, tho not without reluctance, for I can hardly chuse to be out of the ship these ticklish times. I landed safe at 4 p.m. and found Mr Tucker had lost no time nor spared any pains in recommending me. Bryan frankly told me that he was at present engaged with the *Ellis and Robert*, but I might expect the next turn, and proposed my leaving some goods with him now as an introduction, and I might be sure of payment in 10 weeks, but he would not promise before. I easily consented, being glad of an occasion to begin, and doubt not maintaining my hold afterwards. Saw the *Ellis*'s mate on shoar. I find slaves have been very plenty to leeward for he has 23 in the longboat and Bryan says, when the ship went from here she had 240 on board, but the prices, unless he deceives me, are more extravagant there than ever: 7 guns, 7 cags of powder, 4 whole and 5 cut cloths, 4 pans and basons, 2 or 3 kettles, 2 large cases and from 4 to 10 iron bars upon every slave, besides knives, beads and other small articles which together can be little less than 90 ship's bars, besides a double risque; so that upon the whole I beleive I shall determine to stay to windward, because, if by any means I can compleat a cargo this voyage, I shall always [have] a fixed trade for the future. I hear the *Adlington* had near 200 slaves at the time of the insurrection, and that besides the mate, there were 3 or 4 whites killed.

Sunday 19th November. . . . Just about noon departed this life Peter Mackdonald after a week's illness, and who, by Sadlers information was concerned with Swain and Forrester. But he was in a continual delirium from the day before the affair was discovered to me, so that had no opportunity of examining him concerning it. Buryed him at sunsett. I hope every body else that were sick are recovering fast.

['I can sincerely say that I have . . . endeavoured to do my duty by them, without oppression, ill language or any kind of abuse as remembering that I also have a Master in Heaven and that there is no respecter of Persons with him. And I resolve to entertain no personal hatred or ill will. . . . I will treat them with humanity while under my power and not render their confinement unnecessarily grievous, but yet I do not think myself at liberty to dismiss the affair in silence lest encouragement should be thereby given to such attempts. . . .'—From Newton's Diary.]

* * *

Wednesday 22nd November. . . . Arrived the *Brittannia*, Pemberton, from Liverpool, by whom I had a letter from Mr Manesty, directing me not to call at Antigua, but to sail directly for St Christophers when I leave the coast. . . .

* * *

Fryday 1st December. . . . At daylight saw the longboat in shoar. She came on board at 8, brought with her 4 slaves, 2 fine boys and an old man and woman not worth their room which, if possible, I must dispose of again.

['This day has been devoted to serious thoughts. I have had Mr Tucker on board with me for a month; which, in one respect, was no small inconvenience, by breaking in upon my usual times of retirement.'—From *Letters to a Wife*.]

* * *

Monday 11th December. . . . By the favour of Divine Providence made a timely discovery to day that the slaves were forming a plot for an insurrection. Surprized 2 of them attempting to get off their irons, and upon farther search in their rooms, upon the information of 3 of the boys, found some knives, stones, shot, etc., and a cold chissel. Upon enquiry there appeared 8 principally concerned to move in projecting the mischeif and 4 boys in supplying them with the above instruments. Put the boys in irons and slightly in the thumbscrews to urge them to a full confession. We have already 36 men out of our small number.

Tuesday 12th December. . . . In the morning examined the men slaves and punished 6 of the principal, put 4 of them in collars.

* * *

Thursday 14th December. . . . Weighed at daylight, soon after saw a ship to windward, came fast up with us. At 10 I went on board, proved the *Earl of Halifax,* Daniel Thomson, of London, with an engineer, Mr Apperley, and materials for building a new fort at Annamboe. I wrote a letter in form to the captain requesting that, as he had a large and clear ship, he would take charge of my 2 prisoners, Swain and Forrester, and deliver them to the first man of war that offered. With a good deal of persuasion I at last prevailed, sent them on board, and gave bills on the owners for their wages; wrote a letter to the captain of the man of war (whoever it should be) and inclosed the depositions made by Sadler and Coonery. I am very glad to have them out of the ship, for tho I must say they behaved quietly in their confinement, I could not but be in constant alarms, as such a mark of division amongst us was a great encouragement to the slaves to be troublesome, and for ought I know, had it ever come to extremity, they might have joyned hands. . . .

Fryday 15th December. . . . Shipped the balance of the *Duke of Argyle's* account[4] on board the *E. of Hallifax* in 13 men and a man boy slave, upon the following considerations: 1st, because as I propose to take no slaves under 4 feet 2 inches there is a probability of getting an over-proportion of men for our number and perhaps more than we could stow in the room with convenience or look after with safety for we are but weak handed – only 20, myself and boys included, to take care of the ship and man both boats. 2ndly, upon account of the late intended insurrection, in which as they showed their disposition very early, so I took the opportunity to remove the ringleaders out of the ship. 3rdly, to keep the account of the *D. of A.* entirely separate from our present cargoe. And 4thly, I was induced by the best opportunity that could happen, the *Earl of Hallifax* being a very large, roomy vessel, not intended for slaves, and well manned. They promise to keep them all out of irons the whole passage, which I expect will improve them almost to the difference of the freight, which I agreed at 6£ sterling per head, consigned either to Mr Francis Guichard at St Christophers, or to Messrs Thomas Hibbert & Co. in Jamaica as it shall happen. [Both agents for J. Manesty & Co.] Captain Thomson is going directly to Anamboo where he is to discharge his cargoe, and will then proceed without stop to the West Indies. . . .

Saturday 16th December. . . . The *Ellis and Robert*, Jackson, have full slaved excepting a debt he is waiting for from Bryan and his brethren, so think not to stay longer than to write home by him, for we shall but hinder each other and it will be setting an ill example against myself to attempt

[4] Probably slaves bought with the remainder of the 1,000 bars lent to Mr Tucker on 1st April 1751 and the arms and other goods left with him on 19th May when the *Duke of Argyle* sailed for Antigua.

buying slaves they ought to pay, lest it should become my own case when I come to collect from them in my turn. . . .

* * *

Monday 18th December. . . . [*At Cape Mount.*] Found *Ellis* here and understood soon that he has made a breach in the King's promise to me and got 14 slaves from him. However when I went on shoar he gave me a better reception than is common with him, and towards evening showed me 8 slaves out of which I picked 5, viz. 3 girls and 2 boys, all sizeable, and brought them off. Spent the evening on board *Ellis*. He threatens a hard competition, the event of which time will show. I am sure he cannot be much better assorted for them than I am.

* * *

Fryday 22nd December. . . . [*At Rio St Pauls.*] Hoisted the yaul upon deck for she has leaked so much of late that could hardly keep her swimming alongside.

Saturday 23rd December. . . . Carpenter at work upon the yaul. Shall be obliged to shift every foot of plank in her bottom, being quite destroyed by the worms, tho I missed no opportunity of cleaning her, but it appears that the stuff was very bad at first.

Sunday 24th December. . . . Bought a fine boy slave from a little Monserado canoo, but very dear, upwards of 80 bars. I thought the trade bad last voyage, but the price in this place was then under 60. According to this the price about Bassa must be 90 or upwards, perhaps more than 100 for they require 2 guns, 2 cags powder and 2 whole cloths more than I gave here, and an equal quantity (at least) of all other articles. . . .

* * *

Thursday 28th December. . . . The long boat came on board from Grande Bassa. I sent Billinge [second mate] chiefly to satisfy myself of the state and price of slaves. He says the glut we heard so much of is entirely over, the *Brittannia* and *Ranger* having met very few. About Settra Crue there is still plenty (upon the account of a war very probably begun with that view) but extravagantly dear. . . . He brought me a sample of the prices in a woman slave he bought at Bassa, which upon casting up the goods I find cost 96 bars, and I ordered him to get one upon any terms for that reason. That I might not think he gave more than usual, he brought me a list of goods he saw Saunders pay for a man which amounts to 102 bars, and the farther to leeward the dearer still. I think I have sufficient reason not to go down, for setting aside the cost, the assortments in demand there would ruin me soon. How others do I cannot conceive, for I think there was hardly any better stocked than myself. . . .

* * *

Thursday 4th January. . . . At 10 a.m. I went on shoar. Bryan not being upon the beach, I determined to follow him to his town. Did not set out till 5 p.m.; in the interim bought a man and man boy from a stranger and sent them on board. Reached Mr Bryan's 2 hours after dark. . . .

Fryday 5th January. Staid all day with Mr Bryan. He promises if I will stay 14 days to pay off his account and very probably sell me as many more slaves as I can purchase with a good assortment. . . .

Saturday 6th January. In the morning set out from Mr Brian's and got safe on board about 2 p.m. Bought a girl slave by the way. Soon after the longboat came on board, brought 2 men and 1 woman. Arrived the *Swallow*, Lowe, from Liverpool, and anchored by us. Saw 2 other vessels passing down, and fearing that they might otherwise hurt my business at Cape Mount, I went away myself for that place in the longboat just at dark, and about midnight anchored a league short of the town. Was followed hard by the *Swallow*'s boat.

Sunday 7th January. At sunrise landed, was received by the King upon the beach with much seeming kindness. Expected the ship all day but she did not come. The King showed me a number of slaves but I could only pick 6.

Monday 8th January. Early in the morning saw the vessel come down; about 9 she anchored. Mr Welch sent me word that he bought a man yesterday, and was prevented coming down by the cable's bursting when they were weighing, but by the help of the *Swallow*'s boat they saved the anchor. . . .

* * *

Tuesday 23rd January. [*At Mana*.] In the morning went on shoar to see Mr Bryan and hasten his payment. He was up in the country and left word that he had 23 slaves stopped in the path as they were coming down, and he was gone to clear them. . . .

* * *

Thursday 25th January. . . . 6 of our white people and about 5 slaves ill with the flux, but none, I hope, without a prospect of recovery. For these 3 days have omitted giving the slaves pease for breakfast and try them for a while with rice twice a day.

* * *

Tuesday 30th January. . . . I went on shoar seeing a smoke, was shewn 2 men slaves, but not liking them both, could get neither. They say Brian is expected hourly. I begin to think his stay long. I have waited 25 days now instead of 14, but there is no help for it.

Wednesday 31st January. . . . Buryed a girl slave (No. 92). In the afternoon while we were off the deck, William Cooney seduced a woman slave down into the room and lay with her brutelike in view of the whole quarter deck, for which I put him in irons. I hope this has been the first affair of the kind on board and I am determined to keep them quiet if possible. If anything happens to the woman I shall impute it to him, for she was big with child. Her number is 83. . . .

* * *

Saturday 3rd February. . . . Went on shoar, met Brian on the beach, got only 2 men slaves from him. He says I must wait 4 days for the rest yet, for he has been as much disappointed as myself; but paid or not, I think only to stay the return of the longboat.

* * *

Fryday 9th February. . . . When we were putting the slaves down in the evening, one that was sick jumped overboard. Got him in again but he dyed immediately between his weakness and the salt water he had swallowed, tho I imagine he would have lived but a little while being quite worn out. . . .

* * *

Sunday 11th February. . . . Received 1 man slave from Jemmy Cole and 1 man and 2 girls from Bryan, both in full of all demands. Delivered the former his pawn. . . .[5]

[In his Diary Newton mentions a dream he had on 9th February. He thought he had been stung violently by a scorpion and some unknown person applied 'oyl' which gave him ease. This person told him that his dream was 'predictive of something that would happen shortly' but that he should not be afraid as he would suffer no harm. When he woke he related his dream, presumably to his mate or surgeon. He then set out in a boat to see Bryan, but the sea ran high and he did not venture to land. Later, when it was calmer, he started to go ashore with Captain Jennings, but 'some inward hindrance that I could not account for prevailed and I returned to the ship'. On the evening of the 11th, Bryan sent, with the balance of his account, a message to the following effect:

[5] See Introduction, p. xv. In this instance it is probable that Newton lent the dealer goods with which to get slaves, the dealer leaving with Newton a 'free' man (perhaps one of his family) as pawn, or surety.

'. . . he was sorry to have detained me so long for my debts, but had himself been disappointed of his returns out of the country: that he had been very desirous of serving me and till very lately would have been glad if any opportunity of doing so had offered, especially upon the account of Mr Tucker, who recommended me to him, but that I (as he said) well knew I had myself squashed all probability of friendship, *by laying with one of his women when on shoar*; he said he could forgive anything else, but that would stick at his heart as long as he lived: he had not troubled any of my people because they were innocent, and he had sent me the full of what he ow'd me (tho he might have rightfully detained it) for money would make him no recompensation for such an injury; all that he could now do would be to send his longboat after me to Shebar to let Mr Tucker know how unworthy I had behav'd of his confidence, for besides the wrong to him I could not be ignorant that the woman was Mr Tucker's sister, notwithstanding which and his regard for him, she must be miserable as long as she lived, and was now actually in irons upon my account, and by her own confession, with all the circumstances of time and place.'

After expressing his astonishment at this imputation Newton wrote: '. . . it is quite unaccountable from where such a charge could arise. I look upon Mr Bryan to have too much sense and spirit as well as honesty to frame it himself, besides Jennings and my mate say he talks of it with such a mixture of greif and resentment as is not easyly imitated; it is as hard to think how the woman could be induced to accuse herself of a falsehood, which necessarily exposes her to his rage and a variety of punishment: I cannot impute it to revenge having not had a word with her or anyone else and tho such a thing might have been set on foot with a desire of gain (which yet I never met an instance of here before, without a foundation) I can hardly think that Bryan, who is very rich, would stoop to get anything in that manner but imagine he would rather pay a good deal than be mentioned in such a business. For no Spaniard can exceed the heads and better sort of these people either in jealousy or nicety.'

Newton linked this incident with his dream, a warning not to go on shore, 'amongst a mercenary enraged crew and who have poyson always in readiness where they dare not use more open methods of revenge'. Newton drew up a declaration of his 'innocency' and signed it in the presence of Captain Jennings, his own mate and surgeon and sent it to Bryan.]

* * *

Saturday 17th February. [*At Shebar*.] . . . Came down the *Thistle*, Bray, from Gambia. He has about 70 slaves on board in 11 months on the coast. I was informed with a good deal of concern, that Joseph Fellowes, who I shipped second mate with him at Sierra Leon, the 23rd August, deceased in Gambia river. . . .

['He pressed me very much to discharge him having an offer of a second mate's berth. . . . I know not how I shall come off with his wife, but I did it for the best.'—From an unpublished letter to Mrs Newton, dated 6th July 1753.]

* * *

Fryday 23rd February. . . . The boy slaves impeached the men of an intention to rise upon us. Found 4 principally concerned, punished them with the thumb screws and afterwards put them in neck yokes. . . .

Saturday 24th February. . . . Mr Tucker sent me word by his canoo that Monsieur Gervaizeau, commander of a french snow at the Bonanaes, had attacked his shallop on her return from the Susa's, killed one of his people, drove the shallop and the rest on shoar, and plundered her of 5 slaves and 7 cwt of ivory and my punt. This is the man that was cut off in the river when I was here last voyage, and I suppose has done this by way of reprizal, but it is something hard that Mr Tucker only should suffer, when he only had no concern or knowledge of that affair, and to my knowledge redeemed Gervaizeau out of the hands of those who would have murdered him afterwards as an effectual way to stop all enquiries into the fact. However as the shallop was finished by my carpenter, and with the ship's stores and her cargoe put immediately on board by me, and it was known to every body that whatever she bought was engaged to me, I thought I might very lawfully claim her effects as my own, the punt especially which was never yet charged on any account; and besides fearing that my interest and good opinion would much suffer with Mr Tucker and the natives if I set still under these circumstances, and did not show myself as much concerned for his interest, which joyned to my own, as he had all along expressed for mine, and sometimes to his own disadvantage; tho I was very loth to leave the ship at this time and with only one cable, yet I thought it incumbent upon me to attempt speaking with the frenchman before he left the coast. Accordingly put the ship in Mr Welch's charge with orders to proceed for Sierra Leon in 10 days if he did not hear from me, and get the ship ready for the sea. At 2 p.m. put off in the yaul and got safe on shoar in a very small, dangerous canoo, the other being stove. Halled the longboat on shoar directly (she being watering), cleaned her, and ballasted her with iron and camwood, put 4 swivel guns in her and supplied myself with small arms and amunition from Mr Tucker, manned with 6 whites and 2 blacks, being not without apprehension Monsieur might be troublesome. On Sunday morning set out with the flood and that evening reached Jamaica, where I met the shallop and understood my voyage was needless and the Frenchman sailed. But being a good part of the way to the Plantanes, I thought I would go there while I was out, to settle Mr Clow's account, with P.I. It was Tuesday morning before I got there, and the weather detained me till Thursday. Could not come to a settlement with P.I., but beyond my expectation I got from her a new $7\frac{1}{2}$ inch cable of 104 fathoms, which I think well worth the trouble and time of my expedition. . . .

* * *

Monday 5th March. . . . Mr Billinge has been ill these 4 days and continues so. Put 3 hands that I can best trust in the longboat to carry her thro' Sherbro to Sierra-Leon with a letter to desire Mr Staples to procure me rice. I propose to sail as soon as the wind or current will admit, and am afraid to take the longboat round the shoals with me, so many accidents having happened that way by separations.

['I have now been near seven months upon the coast and am yet unable to judge when I shall probably leave it and must expect to make a losing voyage at last. . . . How far two unsuccessful voyages may affect my interest or diminish my expected profits I am tolerably easy—I have placed my dependence higher: I consider my friends and employers as instruments in the hand of God for my good.'—From *Letters to a Wife.*]

* * *

Wednesday 21st March. [*From Shebar for Sierra Leon.*] . . . We begin to be very short of firewood, tho I filled the ship at St Pauls and got all I possibly could at Shebar. Give the slaves bread now for their breakfast for cannot afford them 2 hot meals per day. At least till I see a probability of getting round the shoals. . . .

* * *

Sunday 25th March. . . . Anchored in Frenchmans Bay in 11 fathoms above and without the other ships. Found 9 sail in the bay. . . . In the afternoon went among the ships to enquire for a pilot to carry me up to the factory, but could get none, so must attempt the charge myself. It was with a view of qualifying myself in case of necessity that I went up with Ogilvie[6] when I was here before, and I hope I shall find no great difficulty in it.

Monday 26th March. . . . Weighed at 1 p.m., . . . but the wind failing, could not reach the factory with daylight, so came too at dark. . . .

[6] See 15th September 1752.

Tuesday 27th March. . . . Weighed and run up to the factory without any trouble. Anchored just at noon. . . . Saluted with 5 guns.

* * *

Thursday 29th March. . . . Sold the longboat to the factory for 4 tons rice, an article I am in absolute necessity of, and not to be got here without difficulty. I am to deliver the boat upon my return from Sherbro, where I propose to go in a day or two, to try to dispose of my perishable goods, for there is such a universal stagnation of trade here, and so many pre-engagements, that I cannot expect to get a single slave, tho very well assorted for the place.

Fryday 30th March. Were employed all day in fitting out the longboat, loaded her as deep as she could swim, yet could not put in her all that must be either sold, left behind, or quite spoiled and lost.

Saturday 31st March. This morning set out early in the longboat for Rio Sherbro. (Left directions with Mr Welch to lay the ship on shoar on the spring and clean her, and afterwards make the best dispatch in wooding, watering and preparing for the sea till my return.) Sunday afternoon reached the Plantanes, staid there 2 days and with some trouble perswaded Mr Clow to take such goods as he liked best. . . . April the 5th got to Shebar and put all the rest of the goods on shoar with Mr Tucker, good and bad, whether in demand or not. . . . Before I left him I agreed to run the ship down to the Plantanes from Sierraleon, which I must have done likewise on Mr Clow's account. He promises to send the shallop in 7 days to meet me there with what ever he picks up in that time. . . .Fryday the 13th in the afternoon came into Sierra leon, and at 8 p.m. got safe on board the *African.* Found every body well, by God's blessing, and the ship in greater forwardness and order than I could have expected; top, bottom and sides cleaned, the rice from the factory on board, and all the water, being about 60 buts and puncheons, filled and stowed. Have little now to wait here for but firewood. . . .

* * *

Tuesday 24th April. At sunrise weighed . . . at sunset came too . . . about a mile and a half from the Plantanes. . . .

Wednesday 25th April. Found Mr Tucker's shallop here, received from her one ton of wood, which paid for in cloth according to promise, he complaining when I was at Shebar, that it was hard to take such an odd mixture of spoiling goods without a peice of cloth to assort them. Delivered him likewise a small boy slave (No. 158), which he told me he would send one to redeem, but he now sends word that he has not received a slave since I left him, and he then stripped himself of all to furnish me. Upon the whole I did not think it either grateful or prudent to carry the boy away, which I knew would be a great disadvantage; otherwise I was very loth to part with a slave, tho but a small one, when just upon sailing.

Thursday 26th April. . . . At 2 p.m. weighed with a fresh brease at SW., bound by God's permission for St Christophers. . . .

* * *

[Under date 10th May Newton wrote in his Diary: 'One circumstance I cannot but set down here and which I hope I shall always take pleasure in ascribing to the helping of the God of peace, I mean the remarkable good disposition of the men slaves . . . who seem . . . to have entirely changed their tempers. I was at first continually alarmed with their almost desperate attempts to make insurrections upon us . . . when most quiet they were always watching for opportunity. However from about the end of February they have behaved more like children in one family, than slaves in chains and irons and are really upon all accounts more observant, obliging and considerate than our white people . . . it is true we were not wanting in such methods of guarding against them as custom and prudence suggest, but I hope I shall never be weak and vain enough to think such a guard sufficient: *except the Lord keep the city, the watchman waketh but in vain*, the same may be said of a ship in any circumstances and it is more observably true of a Guineaman.']

* * *

Tuesday 22nd May. . . . [*At sea*.] Have lost 6 whole lines and about twice the number of logs within these few days, the lines being all dry rotten. Are forced now to use fishing lines with a log proportionally smaller. . . .

Wednesday 23rd May. . . . Washed the slaves which the weather has not allowed us to do this fortnight nearly. . . .

Thursday 24th May. . . . Shaved the slaves' fore heads. Buryed a man boy (No. 192) of a pleurisy. . . .

* * *

Fryday 1st June. [*At sea*.] . . . At 6 p.m. saw the land to the SSW., tho could hardly be certain that it was land. Run under easy sail all night . . . and at daylight made the East partof Guadelupa distance about 4 leagues, and Deseada [Désirade], which I suppose was what we saw in the evening, SE. 7 leagues. . . . At 8 saw Antigua and at 10 Monserrat. . . .

Saturday 2nd June. . . . By 1 p.m. stretched close in with the land about half way between Bas-terre and the old road, and at 4 anchored in Sandy point bay in 15 fathoms. Went on shoar, waited on Mr Guichard. Find we came too in foul ground, sent Mr Welsh word to new birth.

Sunday 3rd June. . . . In the morning Mr Guichard went off with me to view the slaves. When came on shoar again, after comparing orders and intelligence, he judged it best for the concern to sell here, if I approved it, without which, he was pleased to say, he would do nothing, tho my letters from the owners referred me wholly to his direction. It seems by all I can learn that this is likely to prove as good a market as any of the neighbouring islands; and as for Jamaica or America, I should be extremely loth to venture so far, for we have had the men slaves so long on board that their patience is just worn out, and I am certain they would drop fast had we another passage to make.[7] Wednesday is appointed for the sale.

Monday 4th June. Fair weather, new birthed a second time. Went to Basse terre. Entered the ship in the secretary's and naval office, and waited upon the Lieutenant General.

Tuesday 5th June. Entered in the custom house at Sandy point. Busy in preparations for landing the slaves.

Wednesday 6th June. Landed the slaves. Sold all to about 20.

Fryday 8th June. Buryed one of the remaining slaves, a man (No. 52).

[Tuesday 12th June. 'I have informed my owners, that I cannot undertake to do any thing upon the windward coast next season, the trade is so overdone. If they will send me, I am ready to go; but I will not be blamed, in case of ill success, for not honestly giving my opinion.' [8]—From *Letters to a Wife*.]

Thursday 14th June. Began to take in sugar.

Saturday 16th June. Went to Basse-terre to buy a cable. . . .

Wednesday 20th June. Finished the sale of the slaves, in all 167, on the ship's account.

[On 3rd July Newton sent his wife 'a piece of paper value £50 sterling money . . . drawn by Francis Guichard on Nicholas Tuite of London, merchant, at 40 days sight dated 14 June and endorsed by me', and three days later, by another ship, 'a bill for £207.3.10 which with that formerly sent you is the amount of my Guinea Commissions and priveledge and so much at least I hope you may compute my profits upon the voyage exclusive of all sorts of expences, charges and loss. I have £23 sterling to pay Mr Lessly's bookkeeper at Antigua for an error in account last voyage which am much surprised at but he has fully con-

[7] Newton had experience of this risk. In 1749 the *Brownlow* left Africa with 218 slaves and sailed to Charleston, Carolina. On the voyage 62 of the slaves died.

[8] When Newton was asked by the Committee of the House of Commons in 1790 if the trade was profitable to the merchants he replied: 'My concern in it was not profitable to my employers: there were some gainful voyages, but the losing voyages were thought more numerous; it was generally considered as a sort of lottery in which every adventurer hoped to gain a prize.'

vinced me that it really is so, therefore shall rectify it with as much pleasure as if the difference was in my own favour.' In these letters (which are unpublished) Newton mentions '7 cags of sweetmeats' he is sending, one containing a pineapple 'such as Mrs Manesty desired me to bring her', another has a pineapple for Mrs Newton from Mrs Guichard, but 'there is no ginger to be got here'. He wrote: 'My time of sailing draws very near . . . nothing is more uncertain than passages, especially homeward from the West Indies: it has been known that a vessel has sailed a month after another, and got home as much before her and no accident happened on either side.']

Monday 9th July. Received on board the last of our homeward cargoe, in all 74 hogsheads, 4 tierces sugar; 23 bags of cotton.

Wednesday 11th July. . . . At 4 p.m. weighed, bound by God's permission for Liverpoole. . . .

* * *

Wednesday 29th August. . . . At 1 p.m. got a pilot, steered NE. for Formby Channel. At 3 made the marks, at 5 entered upon the flats, and about 8 anchored at the Black rock with the best bower in 9 fathoms.

Soli Deo Gloria

The Third Voyage

21ST OCTOBER 1753 – 7TH AUGUST 1754

[A few days after completing the second voyage Newton wrote from Liverpool to Dr David Jennings: 'I have now by God's helping finished a long, troublesome and precarious voyage, with entire satisfaction to myself, my friends and my employers and am now very busy in preparing for another: for it is not in my power to command any respite. . . . I am more than content, in some degree thankful for my lot, which with all its inconveniences I know preferable to many millions of my fellow creatures: yet I still find myself unequal to this fluctuating way of life, where the scene is continually shifting and I am everyday engaged with some new kind of incumbrance.'[1] This letter then discusses a suggestion made by Newton in an earlier letter: 'When it pleased God first to permit me the command and charge of a ship's company, I determined with myself to imitate Joshua's resolution . . . and nothing but an indispensable necessity has prevented me from requiring from all on board a solemn observation of the Sabbath day . . . and here I found myself at a great loss in what manner to regulate our devotions. I could not judge myself equal to the task of conceived prayer before a number of people . . . and no forms that I have met with have been suitable to the particular circumstances of our calling. I was at last forced to take up with the common prayer of the Church of England, which tho it contains many things that I think excellent yet the breaks, the repetitions and indeed the expressions in some places render it, in my opinion, but an indifferent rule for such congregations as mine. . . . To remedy this I venture to compose a short prayer of my own, relating entirely to our own wants and views, which I write down and deliver amongst the rest, always in the same words that the service may be of a peice. I likewise take the liberty of leaving out or changing, to make the whole to the best of my judgement as suitable as possible and tho' after all there are many things that I wished altered, yet it has pleased God so far to bless the sincerity of my intention that there are few moments of my life afford me a more real pleasure than when I am thus attempting the part of a minister to abt. twenty-five people. . . . After this long introduction I come to my proposal . . . a book of advices and devotions might be composed adapted entirely to the business and occasions of seamen.' Newton said that if Jennings could get someone to write and publish such a prayer book at about two shillings a copy he would buy 100 and, 'with previous warning I could get orders for a large number of them in the town of Liverpool'. Newton also mentioned a seventeenth-century book for sailors by a nonconformist minister, John Flavell, en-

[1] Dr Williams's Library, Ref. 38.98.50.

titled, *Navigation Spiritualized or a new compass for seamen consisting of xxxii points of pleasant observations, profitable applications and serious reflections . . . where unto is now added 1. a sober consideration of the sin of drunkness. 2. the harlot's face in the scripture glass. An epistle to seamen sailing heavenwards.* (London, 1682.)

In the ship's company listed in the Journal the name of Captain Job Lewis appears as 'Volunteer and Captain's Commander'. In *An Authentic Narrative,* Newton explained: 'Before I sailed, I met with a young man who had formerly been a midshipman, and my intimate companion on board the *Harwich.* He was, at the time I first knew him, a sober youth: but I found too much success in my unhappy attempts to infect him with libertine principles . . . our conversation frequently turned upon religion; and I was very desirous to repair the mischief I had done him. I gave him a plain account of the manner and reason of my change and used every argument to persuade him to relinquish his infidel schemes. . . . He was then going master to Guinea himself, but before his ship was ready his merchant became a bankrupt. . . . I offered to take him with me as a companion. . . . My view in this was not so much to serve him in his business, as to have an opportunity of debating the point with him at leisure. . . . I had frequent reason to repent it. He was exceedingly profane and grew worse and worse . . . he was not only deaf to my remonstrances himself, but laboured all he could to counteract my influence upon others. . . . He was a sharp thorn in my side . . . at length I had an opportunity upon the coast of buying a small vessel [2] which I supplied with a cargo from my own and gave him the command and sent him away to trade on the ship's account . . . when he found himself at liberty from under my eye, he gave a hasty loose to every appetite and his violent irregularities, joined to the heat of the climate, soon threw him into a malignant fever, which carried him off in a few days. He died convinced, but not changed. The account I had from those who were with him was dreadful. His rage and despair struck them all with horror; and he pronounced his own fatal doom before he expired, without any appearance that he either *hoped* or *asked* for mercy.']

Officers and seamen on board the *African,* second voyage
Commenced Pay 21st October 1753

Names	*Quality*	*Wages per month*	*Dead, run or discharged*
John Newton	Master	£5	
Alexander Welsh	1st Mate	4	Discharged 22 Febry *Racehorse*
William Brown	Surgeon	3. 10	

[2] The *Racehorse.*

James Billinge	2nd Mate	3	
Joseph Taylor	3rd Mate		
Heton Wooler	Boatswain	2. 7. 6	Discharged 19 June
Thomas Hawkes	Carpenter	3. 10	
John Megan	Cooper	2. 5	
Joseph White	Gunner	1. 12. 6	Discharged 14 Febry *Racehorse*
Thomas Wilson	Steward	1	
James Richardson	Fore the mast	1. 8	
Thomas Williamson	do.	1. 8	Discharged 1 April *Racehorse*
William Heberon	do.	1. 8	Discharged 1 April *Racehorse*
George Manwaring	do.	1. 8	
James Allen	do.	1. 8	Discharged 1 April *Racehorse*
William Morrison	do.	1. 8	Discharged 1 April *Racehorse*
James Smith	do.	1. 8	
Manuel Antonio	do.	1. 8	Run in Sherbro March
John Shestnassy [*sic*] [1]	do.	1. 8	
Charles Garnish	do.	1. 8	
Henry Davy	do.	1. 8	Discharged 1 April *Racehorse*
Robert Rose	do.	1. 8	
Thomas Parry	do.	1. 8	
John Bridson	do.	1. 8	Discharged 1 April *Racehorse*
Robert Cropper	Ship's Apprentice		Discharged 1 April *Racehorse*
James Morgave	do.		
Jonathan Ireland	do.		Discharged 1 April *Racehorse*

Captain Job Lewis, Volunteer and Captain's Commander, deceased at Mana the 17th February

John Cardue
Francis Carren } Shipped at Cape Mount 28 Decr. Run at St Kitts 2nd June

[1] Newton had difficulty in spelling Shaughnessy.

Officers & Seamen on board the African, second voyage

Commenced pay	Names	Quality	Wages £	Dead run or discharged
1753	John Newton	Master	£5.–	
21st October	Alexander Welsh	1st Mate	4.–.–	Discharg'd 22 Febry Racehorse
	√ William Brown	Surgeon	3.10.–	D
	√ James Billinge	2nd Mate	3.–	
	√ Joseph Taylor	3d Mate		
	√ Heton Wooler	Boatswain	2.7.6	Discharg'd 19 June
	√ Thomas Hawkes	Carpenter	3.10.–	
	√ John Magan	Cooper	2.5.–	Disch. 24 Febry Racehorse
	√ Joseph White	Gunner	1.12.6	Ran
	√ Thomas Wilson	Steward	1.–	
	√ James Richardson	Fore ye mast	1.8.–	
	√ Thoms. Williamson	do.	1.8	Disch'd 1 April Racehorse
	√ Willm. Hebiron	do.	1.8	disch'd 1 April Racehorse
	√ George Manwaring	do.	1.8	
	√ James Allen	do.	1.8	disch'd 1 April racehorse
	√ Willm. Morrison	do.	1.8	disch'd 1 April Racehorse
	√ James Smith	do.	1.8	
	√ Manuel Antonio	do.	1.8	Run in Shebro March
	√ John Shornasy	do.	1.8	
	√ Charles Garnish	do.	1.8	
	√ Henry Davy	do.	1.8	disch'd April 1 Racehorse
	√ Robert Rose	do.	1.8	
	√ Thomas Parry	do.	1.8	
	√ John Bridson	do.	1.8	disch'd 1 April Racehorse
	Robert Cropper	Ship's Apprentice		disch'd 1 April Racehorse
	James Morgan	do.		
	Jonathan Ireland	do.		disch'd 1 April Racehorse

Captain Job Lewis, Volunteer & Captain's Commander. Deceased at Mana ye 17th February

John Cordner, Francis Carrell } Shipp'd at Cape Mount 28 Decr. run at St. Kitts 2d June

African, second voyage

[A comparison with wages in an East India Company ship at this time is interesting, though it must be remembered that some officers in the slave trade had a share of profits and there were probably perquisities in the East India trade. Newton's share of profits on his second voyage totalled £257.3.11. The first mate had a much smaller share and it was common for surgeons to be paid head money according to the number of slaves who survived the voyage. The East India Company ship, *Lord Anson*, with a ship's company of 115, had a pay roll as follows: captain £10 per month, chief mate £5, second mate £4, third mate £3, fourth mate £2, fifth mate 30/-, two sixth mates 23/-, purser £2, surgeon £3, boatswain 55/-, gunner 55/-, carpenter 70/-, surgeon's mate 30/-, carpenter's mate 50/-, seamen 23/-. Contributions to Seamen's Hospital, Greenwich, were deducted from all these amounts before payment.]

Laus Deo

Journal of a voyage intended, by God's permission, in the snow, African, *from Liverpoole to the Windward Coast of Africa.* 1753, etc.

Sunday 21st October. At 6 a.m. weighed with a light brease from the rock. . . .

* * *

Fryday 23rd November. . . . In the afternoon discovered John Megan, cooper, and James Allen had been guilty of barratry, the former in broaching a cask of ale reserved for cabbin use, and filling it up with water, and both in secreting some bottles of snuff, part of the cargoe, for their own use. Put them in irons, and in the morning, the facts being fully proved, discharged them at the gangway; ordered J. Allen 11 lashes and the cooper 17[1] as being an officer, by which his offence seemed more aggravated. Had a third in confinement on suspicion, but dismissed him scot-free.

* * *

Sunday 2nd December. . . . At daylight saw Cape St Anne and the islands . . . and at 11 saw the land of Shebar. . . . At 5 p.m. passed 4 vessels at anchor off the bar. Spoke one, the *Penelope*, Wyat, of Liverpool. The others are the *Minerva*, Colhoun, the *Success*, Ingledue, a brig, and the *Racehorse*, snow, lately cut off and recovered from the natives in the Susas. . . .

* * *

[1] Newton first wrote '12' and '18'.

Tuesday 4th December. . . . Went to the beach with Captain Lewis in the yaul. Found Mr Tucker just arrived. . . . In the afternoon the ship weighed and came in with the sea brease, anchored in 15 fathoms . . . fired 7 guns. . . . The rest of the day passed in feasting, firing and other demonstrations of joy.

* * *

Fryday 7th December. . . . The *Adventure*, Beatson, of London, who had been near 5 months on the coast when I left it, was run on shoar last Wednesday morning by the slaves in an insurrection about 3 leagues below the bar and totally lost, but the people, all but 1 killed and 1 wounded, got off on board Captain Colhoun, who was going downwards at that time. . . .

* * *

[*Monday 10th December*. 'I arrived in safety at Shebar, the second instant, found my friend Harry [Tucker] well and very glad to see me. Your picture, if it could speak, might tell you how pleased his *first* lady was with your present; for she dressed herself in it before *you,* and seemed to think that in her new attire, she might stand in competition with you. I believe you will smile at her vanity and think I pay you no great compliment, in preferring your *picture* to her *reality*.' From *Letters to a Wife*.]

* * *

Fryday 21st December. . . . Corrected the carpenter with a catt for having behaved very mutinously in my abseence, daring the officers and refusing his duty; likewise for making a disturbance on shoar on Wednesday, when I sent for him to cut stantients, where he grossly abused Mr Billinge and swore he would not proceed in the ship. The barricado not being built I could not afford to put him in irons. Mem: gave him 2 dozen stripes. [Entry on Sunday 23rd: 'Carpenter at work on the barricado.']

* * *

Wednesday 26th December. [*At Cape Mount*]. . . . Came down a very large Dane who I beleive will hinder us much here. Came up from to leeward the *Patience*, sloop, Holland, of St Kitts; he has 32 slaves on board in about 2 months. He gives a strange account of trade down below, and that the price of slaves is run up to 120 bars and upwards.

* * *

Fryday 28th December. . . . Bartered with Holland for 3 hogsheads of rum at 3/9 per gallon. . . . Shipped John Cardue and Francis Carren.

* * *

Sunday 30th December. . . . Went on board the *Success* to treat with Engledue [2] about his snow, *Racehorse*, now lying at Shebar. Could not come to terms, left him and in the evening sent for him to supper, but parted again without concluding any thing. As my orders are to leave the coast in April, I think, considering the present state of trade, nothing but the purchase of this vessel can save our voyage from utter ruin, as it is highly probable I shall not have less than 1000 £ goods on hand at the time of departure, which will be perhaps never recovered if left in the country, and surely spoiled if carryed off; but may be put on board her, especially as I have Captain Lewis free to take charge of her to as much an advantage as if I staid on the coast myself, and will be upon the spot to purchase camwood without competition when Grayson goes off. She is about 40 or 45 tons, spanish bottom, and rebuilt 3 years since in London, new sheathed, and seems in every respect a good vessel. The only difficulty is want of her papers, which were all lost when she was cut off, of which accident and the manner there is a deposition on board the *Crown*, man of war, Captain Barrington, and Ingledue has an absolute letter of attorney impowering him to sell.

Monday 31st December. In the morning early paid Engledue another visit, and at last struck the bargain for 130 £ sterling in a bill on Jill & Compy, with my own security for acceptance. Sent for Roberts and Hammond [3] to witness the agreement. Were employed most of the day in writing, signing and delivering on both sides. Borrowed his yaul to send people up to take possesion of her, and gave Captain Lewis a written appointment to command her.

Tuesday 1st January 1754. At 4 a.m. Captain Lewis and 4 hands went away for Shebar to undertake his charge and bring her down to us that she may be fitted out with a cargo to lye to windward of Cape Mount while I am to leeward. . . .

* * *

Fryday 4th January. [*At Rio Junque*.] . . . Sent Mr Taylor [third mate] in the yaul . . . with goods for 4 slaves, that is to say, with 420 bars for 4 slaves which even in my time would have purchased 10. . . .

Saturday 5th January. Sent the punt for Yellow Will, he came off and staid

[2] Nics Owen mentions a Captain Engledue who 'refused the king his custom, which has bred a great palaver between the king and all the whites so that it's dangerous to pass or repass in the river. It has cost Mr Tucker 4 or 5 bars and is not finished yet' [10th January 1757–8]. Three days later he wrote: 'I have been on board of Capt. Engledo today, where I found him employed in making a curious piece of shell work in his cabbin upon an old picture. Tomorrow I entend to imatate him as nigh as my abilities will alow, as we have great numbers of shells upon the beetch.'

[3] Roberts was master of the *Spencer*, and Hammond master of a brig from Rhode Island.

all day: fired 6 guns and made him some presents, whether it will quit cost I know not but must do as others or be quite ruined. Came down the *Jesse* who is like to be a strong competitor here, by having redeemed and brought back one of the people that the *Adlington* carryed off. Yellow Will says his son, but I question it....

* * *

Thursday 10th January. [*At Grande Bassa.*] ... The yaul ... brought a man slave which cost 120 bars, through the positiveness of competitors. One of my people had been 2 days walk in the woods to look at him, so they were determined not to be outbid, which in this particular case I commended them for, tho it will never do to continue in this way of giving nearly what slaves will fetch in the West Indies, exclusive of freight and commissions, which if reckoned with all other charges here and there, brings a slave to £22 sterling on board, besides the tediousness of trade and the risque of mortality....

* * *

Fryday 18th January. [*At Rio Junque.*] ... Compleated the outfit and cargoe of the *Racehorse entirely.* Sent the carpenter to stay in her for one cruze, to put everything in as good order as possible. At 10 p.m. Captain Lewis went on board. ... He is at the head of about 3200 bars, well assorted....

* * *

Sunday 27th January. [*At Little Sestors.*] In the morning fired 3 guns and made a signal for canoos, but only one came off all day (my old trader, Ben Johnson) to tell me that every body was engaged, the country full of goods, and he could not give me any encouragement. This has been thought for 3 years past the best place of trade on this coast, but now like all the rest entirely overdone. Captain Jackson and I agreed to go together down to Grand Sestors and Cape Palmas to take our chance of trade, and assist and protect each other, for they have got such a head in their first villainy thereabouts, that it is judged precarious for a single ship to venture near them....

* * *

Tuesday 5th February. [*At Crue Settera.*] ... Fired 2 guns for trade, but in vain; the beach is full of longboats. ... Captain Boucher [Master of the *Fortune* of Bristol] came on board; he tells me he has been obliged to give 12 guns, 12 cags powder, 2 and 3 ps basts with other things to the amount of 19 £ sterling for a single slave, which I am resolved not to do upon any consideration.

Wednesday 6th February. . . . I think to go down no farther, nor wait to leeward any longer, as time runs on fast and it is likely by that time I can reach Shebar, stopping by the way for wood, water and debts at different places, and sometimes waiting a chance of trade, the month of March will be far advanced if not quite ended, and my orders are to leave the coast in April, which I shall if possible comply with literally, and with chearfulness now I have secured the *Race-horse* to take all our goods. Otherwise I know not which would be most disadvantageous, to go or stay.

* * *

Wednesday 13th February. . . . An excessive dark, dismal night. At 9 had another tornado, which expected would clear up the weather, but at 11 were overtaken by a third, which proved one of the most violent I have seen. It blew nearly up the coast. Could barely suffer a foresail, under which the vessel hurried along at an unusual rate. In the height of the squall the yaul broke the best chain on board and 2 ropes, and was out of sight in a moment. It was impossible to attempt any thing to save her or to recover her, for it was near half an hour after ere we could venture to bring the wind upon the quarter, and the night so close, there was no seeing 10 yards anyway, unless in the glare of the lightning. . . .

* * *

Monday 18th February. [*At Little Sesters.*] . . . The Longboat came down from Sherbro and the Plantanes, brought 17 slaves, viz. 3 men, 4 boys, 2 women and eight girls; 2 being purchased from H. Tucker, 9 from Mr Clow and 1 from Capt. Lewis, who has been very ill; likewise 2 tons of Camwood. Mr Billinge came on board ill, likewise he says that Lewis has about 10 more slaves.

* * *

Thursday 21st February. . . . Ran up to Grande Bassa, anchored at 5 p.m. in 13 fathoms, fired 3 guns. Soon after saw the *Racehorse*. As she drew nearer she began to fire minute guns, and perceived her colours half mast, a melancholy signal of Captain Lewis' death. At 7 she anchored near us. Mr Tayler came on board, informed me that he deceased the 17th at Mana, after a week's illness, that he buried him the same day in the offing according to his own desire, and then came away immediately. As our intimacy had been so long and so great, I expected to meet some intimation among his papers, how he would have his effects disposed of, but could find nothing of the kind. Mr Tayler and one of the people, William Hebbard, agreed in a verbal declaration he made about the middle of his illness, by which he left the greater part of his cloathes to the officers, Jo White and the 2 lads that had sailed with him in the *Grampus*, a mourning ring, value 5 guineas to Mr and Mrs Manesty and myself, and 150 £ apeice to his 2 sisters. Went on board with Mr Welsh and tendered him the command. He desired a few hours to think of it, but as it [is] absolutely [in] the interest of the concern, I expect he will not long hesitate, for she will be as great a charge as a vessel immediately from England.

Fryday 22nd February. . . . In the morning put Mr Welsh in posession. . . . I have only Joseph White to go as mate of the *Racehorse* being obliged for strong reasons to displace Mr Tayler and take him on board the *African*. . . . In the afternoon distributed the most of Captain Lewis's apparel, etc., in the most agreeable manner to his intention I could gather from what I heard or knew of him. Took on board the slaves he purchased while he was well, 3 men, 4 boys, 2 girls, besides the boy that came in the longboat from him; likewise 6 cwt camwood, which it seems is not yet paid for. Mem: the cargoe is debtor to his account £8.10 for sundry things of his own he sold in trade amounting to 34 bars. Fired 6 minute guns at sunrise. . . .

* * *

Wednesday 27th February. . . . Have had no news from Jo. Gray yet about my slaves, it is lucky I only have goods ashoar for 4 for I am likely to lose them all. Indeed it was much against my will I trusted for any but thought it incumbent on me to make the essay, as every body else did it without scruple.

Thursday 28th February. [*At Rio Junque*.] . . . Wrote letters to go home by Captain Grayson, likewise one to Mr Clow to recommend Mr Welsh and the *Racehorse* to him if I should not have time to see him myself, and to beg he would give me one more lot of trade before I go off.

* * *

Wednesday 20th March. [*At Cape Mount*.] . . . I was in hopes to have seen Mr Bryan to accomodate, if possible, our foolish difference, but he is not come down from Bassa yet; left a letter on board the *Ellis and Robert* for him. [4]

* * *

Wednesday 27th March. [*At Shebar*.] . . . Mr Dickenson in the *Grayhound's* yaul was cut off last week by Robin Will at Kittam, himself and his 2 white people all murdered, and the boat halled on shoar. . . .

* * *

Friday 5th April. . . . Mem: Manuel Antonio, a Portuguese sailor, who shipped with us at Liverpool, run away from the boat the last time she was at Cachugo. He pretends for ill usage, but every officer on board can witness he never was struck by any one. The true reason it seems by Mr

[4] For this foolish difference, see page 75.

Billinge's account is having been detected stealing some knives and tobacco out of the boat.

Saturday 6th April.... The longboat came on board, took the wood out of her and delivered her with all her materials . . . to Mr Welsh; put all the remaining goods and stores on board him. Settled all accounts with him, and took his receipt for 8169 bars on ship's account, and the several stores and provisions. [Newton valued this cargo at 'about a thousand pounds'. From *Letters to a Wife*.] Marked him 6 slaves, 2 men and 4 boys, one priveledge, the rest in payment for his adventure yet unsold, which I added to his new invoyce, and the camwood he rceived from Mr Clow for guns and powder, being 1 tons 12 cwt; signed bills of lading for his slaves consigned to myself at £6 per head. Settled all the people's accounts that are to stay with him, and paid them their ballance in bills on the owners. Shipped them on board the *Racehorse* at 35 s. per month.... In the evening unmored.

People remaining on the coast in the *Racehorse*.

Alexander Welsh . . Master
Joseph White . . Mate
William Heberon . . Boatswain
if behaves well

John Bridson James Allen Thomas Williams William Morrison Henry Davy	Fore the mast	Robert Cropper Jonathan Ireland	Ship's Apprentices

Sunday 7th April. . . . Weighed, bound by God's permission to St Christophers....

* * *

[On 10th April Newton wrote in his Diary: 'I think the last season upon the coast has been more remarkable for deaths and misfortunes than any I have been in before and yet to myself it proved the most pleasant and free from uneasiness.... I propose to dedicate this day to recollect and acknowledge the mercies and blessings of my past life and especially since I last left England.']

* * *

Tuesday 23rd April. I have been indisposed of a fever and not capable of observing till today. I have little or no correction to make if my observation is good, but my eyes were very weak. I hope I am now (by God's blessing) recovering.

* * *

Fryday 17th May. [*At sea.*] ... The brig came up and spoke us, the *Harlequin*, Mansfield, of Lima from Madeira for Antigua. Hoisted out his boat and spared me some fresh provisions and wine. He does not reckon himself to the westward of 50° and has been only 15 days out....

Saturday 18th May. ... Upon further talk with Captain Mansel, find he reckons his longitude from the Lizard, and is consequently far to the westward of me, instead of the eastward as I imagined....

* * *

Monday 20th May. ... At daylight made Antigua right a head and very near....

Tuesday 21st May. ... Anchored in Basse-terre road. Had afterwards continual rain. Went on shoar, took horse and waited upon Mr Guichard at Sandy Point.

Wednesday he returned with me and it was concluded to run the ship down to Sandy point, which we accordingly did on Thursday; anchored there and mored a little after sunsett.

[Newton wrote from St Christophers to Dr Jennings 7th June: '... I have been preserved safe thro' all the events of another season in Africa; a season the most remarkably fatal and disastrous to numbers of any I have seen, yet I, as formerly, was spared when many of equal views fell before me, behind me, on my right hand and on my left, and even in my sight. It is true indeed my sanguine views with regard to profit, with which I first sat out here have something failed me, yet I think your kind wishes in your last are accomplished, for I can say in my measure that I have all and abound, and hope, I have reason to look upon this as a pleasant and gainful voyage and the best hitherto I have ever made. Upon this head I cannot omit mentioning what I look upon as a special mercy and favour which I have lately received; like Elijah I was ready to think I was in a manner serving my God alone, with respect to the generality of those of my own profession and the inhabitants of this dry and barren land where there are hardly any waters, any streams of gospel communion and experiences to be found, but I have met with a brother sailor, a brother captain too, whose acquaint I esteem beyond any temporal advantage that could have fallen to me: as he is an acquaintance of yours I shall only tell you his name is Alex Clunie.... I hope to sail for Liverpool within 14 days.' [5]

[The *African* sailed from Sandy Point on 20th June 1754 and reached Liverpool on 7th August 1754.

[5] Dr Williams's Library, Ref. 38.98.54.

[The last entry in the Journal is on a separate page.]

		Whites	Died	Blacks	D'yd
1750	Duke Argyle	30	7	174	28
1752	African	27	1	207	[no entry]
1753	African	27	none	87	none

[On 18th August 1754, Newton wrote from Warrington of his last voyage: 'I had the pleasure of returning thanks, in all the churches [of Liverpool], for an African voyage performed without any disaster, or the loss of a single man for Captain L**** was fixed in another vessel, some time before his death. This was much noticed, and spoken of in the town; and I believe it is the first instance of the kind.' From *Letters to a Wife.*]

In giving evidence to the Privy Council, in the year 1789, Newton stated that on this voyage he sailed with 'only 90 slaves instead of 220 originally intended', and added: 'Had I remained there till I had compleated my purchase there is little doubt but I should have shared largely in the mortality so usual in vessels crowded with slaves.'

[In *An Authentic Narrative,* Newton described how he came to give up the slave trade: 'I arrived safe in L——, August 1754. My stay at home was intended to be but short and by the beginning of November I was again ready for the sea [in a ship named the *Bee*]: but the Lord saw fit to overrule my design. During the time I was engaged in the slave trade, I never had the least scruple as to its lawfulness. I was upon the whole satisfied with it, as the appointment Providence had worked out for me; yet it was, in many respects, far from eligible. It is, indeed, accounted a genteel employment and is usually very profitable, though to me it did not prove so, the Lord, seeing that a large increase of wealth would not be good for me. However, I considered myself a sort of gaoler or turnkey and I was sometimes shocked with an employment that was perpetually conversant with chains, bolts and shackles. In this view I had often petitioned in my prayers that the Lord (in his own time) would be pleased to fix me in a more humane calling, and (if it might be) place me where I might have more frequent converse with his people and ordinances and be freed from those long separations from home which very often were hard to bear. My prayers were now answered, though in a way I little expected. I now experienced another sudden unforeseen change of life. I was within two days of sailing and to all appearance in good health as usual; but in the afternoon, as I was sitting with Mrs N*****, by ourselves, drinking tea and talking over past events, I was in a moment seized with a fit, which deprived me of sense and motion and left no other sign of life than that of breathing.—I suppose it was of the apoplectic kind. It lasted about an hour; and when I recovered it left a pain and dizziness in my head which continued with such symptoms as induced the physicians to judge it would not be safe or prudent for me to proceed on the voyage. Accordingly by the advice of my friend to whom the ship belonged I resigned the command the day before she sailed; and thus I was unexpectedly called from that service and freed from a share of the future consequences of that voyage which proved extremely calamitous. The person who went in my room, most of the officers, and many of the crew, died and the vessel was brought home with great difficulty.']

THOUGHTS
UPON THE
AFRICAN SLAVE TRADE

by JOHN NEWTON
Rector of St. Mary Woolnoth

MATT vii 12

All things whatsoever ye would that men should do to you, do ye even so to them; for this is the law and the prophets.

Homo Sum ——

LONDON

PRINTED FOR J. BUCKLAND IN PATER-NOSTER ROW; AND
J. JOHNSON, IN ST. PAULS CHURCHYARD

M. DCC. LXXXVIII

THE nature and effects of that unhappy and disgraceful branch of commerce, which has long been maintained on the coast of Africa, with the sole and professed design of purchasing our fellow creatures, in order to supply our West India islands and the American colonies, when they were ours, with slaves, is now generally understood. So much light has been thrown upon the subject by many able pens, and so many respectable persons have already engaged to use their utmost influence for the suppression of a traffic which contradicts the feelings of humanity, that it is hoped this stain of our national character will be soon wiped out.

If I attempt, after what has been done to throw my mite into the public stock of information, it is less from an apprehension that my interference is necessary, than from a conviction that silence, at such a time and on such an occasion, would, in me, be criminal. If my testimony should not be necessary or serviceable, yet, perhaps, I am bound in conscience to take shame to myself by a public confession, which, however sincere, comes too late to prevent or repair the misery and mischief to which I have, formerly, been accessary.

I hope it will always be a subject of humiliating reflection to me, that I was once an active instrument in a business at which my heart now shudders. My headstrong passions and follies plunged me, in early life, into a succession of difficulties and hardships, which at length, reduced me to seek a refuge among the natives of Africa. There, for about the space of eighteen months, I was in effect, though without the name, a captive, and slave myself; and was depressed to the lowest degree of human wretchedness. Possibly I should not have been so completely miserable, had I lived among the natives only, but it was my lot to reside with white men; for at that time several persons of my own colour and language were settled upon that part of the Windward coast which lies between Sierra Leon and Cape Mount; for the purpose of purchasing and collecting slaves, to sell to the vessels that arrived from Europe.

This is a bourn from which few travellers return, who have once determined to venture upon a temporary residence there; but the good providence of God, without my expectation, and almost against my will, delivered me from those scenes of wickedness and woe; and I arrived at Liverpool, in May 1748. I soon revisited the place of my captivity, as mate of a ship, and, in the year 1750, I was appointed commander; in which capacity I made three voyages to the Windward coast for slaves.

I first saw the coast of Guinea, in the year 1745, and took my last leave of it in 1754. It was not, intentionally, a farewel; but, through the mercy of God, it proved so. I fitted out for a fourth voyage, and was upon the point of sailing, when I was arrested by a sudden illness, and I resigned the ship to another captain.

Thus I was unexpectedly freed from this disagreeable service. Disagreeable I had long found it; but I think I should have quitted it sooner, had I considered it as I now do, to be unlawful and wrong. But I never had a scruple upon this head at the time; nor was such a thought once suggested to me by any friend. What I did I did ignorantly; considering it as the line of life which Divine Providence had allotted me, and having no concern, in point of conscience, but to treat the slaves, while under my care, with as much humanity as a regard to my own safety would admit.

The experience and observation of nine years, would qualify me for being a competent witness upon this subject, could I safely trust to the report of memory, after an interval of more than thirty-three years. But, in the course of so long a period, the ideas of past scenes and transactions grow indistinct; and I am aware, that what I have seen, and what I have only heard related, may, by this time, have become so insensibly blended together, that, in some cases, it may be difficult for me, if not impossible, to distinguish them with absolute certainty. It is, however, my earnest desire, and will, therefore, engage my utmost care, that I may offer nothing in writing, as from my own knowledge, which I could not cheerfully, if requisite, confirm upon oath.

That part of the African shore, which lies between the river Sierra Leon, lat. 8° 30′ N. and Cape Palmas, is usually known by the name of the Windward, or Grain Coast. The extent (if my recollection does not fail me) is about one hundred and fifty leagues. There is a fort upon Benee Island, in Sierra Leon, which formerly belonged to the old African company: they also had a fort on an island in the river Sherbro; but the former was in private hands, and of the latter, scarcely the foundations were visible, when I first went to Africa. There is no fort or factory upon this coast, under the sanction of our government; but there were, as I have said, and probably still are, private traders resident at Benee Island, at the Bananoes, and at the Plantanes. The former of these is about twelve, and the latter twenty leagues, from Sierra Leon to the southeast.

By these persons, the trade is carried on, in boats and shallops, thirty or forty leagues to the northward, in several rivers lying within the shoals of Rio Grande. But the most northerly place for shipping is Sierra Leon, and the business there, and in that neighbourhood, is chiefly transacted with the white men: but from Sherbro to Cape Palmas, directly with the natives. Though I have been on the Gold Coast, and beyond it as far as Cape Lopez, in the latitude of one or two degrees south, I profess no knowledge of the African trade but as it was conducted on the Windward Coast when I was concerned in it.

I am not qualified, and if I were, I should think it rather unsuitable to my present character as a minister of the Gospel, to consider the African slave trade merely in a political light. This disquisition more properly belongs to persons in civil life. Only thus far my character as a minister will allow, and perhaps require me to observe, that the best human policy is that which is connected with a reverential regard to Almighty God, the supreme governor of the earth. Every plan, which aims at the welfare of a nation, in defiance of his authority and laws, however apparently wise, will prove to be essentially defective, and, if persisted in, ruinous. The righteous Lord loveth righteousness, and he has engaged to plead the cause and vindicate the wrongs of the oppressed. It is righteousness that exalteth a nation; and wickedness is the present reproach, and will, sooner or later, unless repentance intervene, prove the ruin of any people.

Perhaps what I have said of myself may be applicable to the nation at large. The slave trade was always unjustifiable; but inattention and interest prevented, for a time, the evil from being perceived. It is otherwise at present; the mischiefs and evils connected with it have been, of late years, represented with such undeniable evidence, and are now so generally known, that I suppose there is hardly an objection can be made to the wish of thousands, perhaps of millions, for the suppression of this trade, but upon the ground of political expedience.

Though I were even sure that a principal branch of the public revenue depended upon the African trade (which I apprehend is far from being the case), if I had access and influence, I should think myself bound to say to Government, to Parliament, and to the nation, 'It is not lawful to put it into the treasury, because it is the price of blood' (Matt xxvii. 6).

I account an intelligent farmer to be a good politician in this sense; that if he has a large heap of good corn, he will not put a small quantity, that is damaged, to the rest, for the sake of increasing the heap. He knows that such an addition would spoil the whole. God forbid that any supposed profit or advantage which we can derive from the groans, and agonies, and blood of the poor Africans, should draw down his heavy curse upon all that we might, otherwise, honourably and comfortably possess.

For the sake of method, I could wish to consider the African trade,—first, with regard to the effect it has upon our own people; and secondly, as it concerns the blacks, or, as they are more contemptuously styled, the negro slaves, whom we purchase upon the coast. But these two topics are so interwoven together, that it will not be easy to keep them exactly separate.

1. The first point I shall mention is surely of political importance, if the lives of our fellow-subjects be so; and if a rapid loss of seamen deserves the attention of a maritime people. This loss, in the African trade, is truly alarming. I admit, that many of them are cut off in their first voyage, and consequently, before they can properly rank as seamen; though they would have been seamen if they had lived. But the neighbourhood of our sea-

ports is continually drained of men and boys to supply the places of those who die abroad; and if they are not all seamen, they are all our brethren and countrymen, subjects of the British government.

The people who remain on ship-board, upon the open coast, if not accustomed to the climate, are liable to the attack of an inflammatory fever, which is not often fatal, unless the occurrence of unfavorable circumstances makes it so. When this danger is over, I think they might probably be as healthy as in most other voyages, provided they could be kept from sleeping in the dews, from being much exposed to the rain, from the intemperate use of spirits, and especially from women.

But considering the general disposition of our sailors, and the nature of the slave trade, these provisoes are of little more significance than if I should say upon another occasion, that Great Britain would be a happy country, *provided* all the inhabitants were wise and good. The sailors *must be* much exposed to the weather; especially on the Windward coast, where a great part of the cargo is procured by boats, which are often sent to the distance of thirty or forty leagues, and are sometimes a month before they return. Many vessels arrive upon the coast before the rainy season, which continues from about May to October, is over; and if trade be scarce, the ships which arrive in the fair or dry season, often remain till the rains return, before they can complete their purchase. A proper shelter from the weather, in an open boat, when the rain is incessant, night and day, for weeks and months, is impracticable.

I have, myself, in such a boat, been, five or six days together, without, as we say, a dry thread about me, sleeping or waking. And, during the fair season, tornadoes, or violent storms of wind, thunder, and heavy rain, are very frequent, though they seldom last long. In fact, the boats seldom return, without bringing some of the people ill of dangerous fevers or fluxes, occasioned either by the weather, or by unwholsome diet, such as the crude fruits and palm wine, with which they are plentifully supplied by the natives.

Strong liquors, such as brandy, rum, or English spirits, the sailors cannot often procure, in such quantities as to hurt them; but they will if they can; and opportunities sometimes offer, especially to those who are in the boats: for strong liquor being an article much in demand, so that without it scarcely a single slave can be purchased, it is always at hand. And if what is taken from the casks or bottles that are for sale, be supplied with water, they are as full as they were before. The blacks who buy the liquor, are the losers by the adulteration; but often the people who cheat them are the greatest sufferers.

The article of women, likewise, contributes largely to the loss of our seamen. When they are on shore, they often, from their known thoughtless imprudence, involve themselves, on this account, in quarrels with the natives, and, if not killed upon the spot, are frequently poisoned. On ship-board they may be restrained, and in some ships they are; but such restraint is far from being general. It depends much upon the disposition and attention of the captain. When I was in the trade I knew several commanders of African ships who were prudent, respectable men, and who maintained a proper discipline and regularity in their vessels; but there were too many of a different character. In some ships, perhaps in the most, the licence allowed in this particular, was almost unlimited. Moral turpitude was seldom considered, but they who took care to do the ship's business, might, in other respects, do what they pleased. These excesses, if they do not induce fevers, at least render the constitution less able to support them; and lewdness, too frequently, terminates in death.

The risk of insurrections is to be added. These, I believe, are always meditated; for the men slaves are not easily reconciled to their confinement and treatment; and, if attempted, they are seldom suppressed without considerable loss; and sometimes they succeed, to the destruction of a whole ship's company at once. Seldom a year passes, but we hear of one or more such catastrophes; and we likewise hear, sometimes of Whites and Blacks involved, in one moment, in one common ruin, by the gunpowder taking fire, and blowing up the ship.

How far the several causes I have enumerated, may respectively operate, I cannot say; the fact, however, is sure, that a great number of our seamen perish in the slave trade. Few ships, comparatively, are either blown up, or totally cut off; but some are. Of the rest, I have known some that have lost half their people, and some a larger proportion. I am far from saying, that it is always, or even often, thus; but, I believe I shall state the matter sufficiently low, if I suppose, that at least one-fifth part of those who go from England to the coast of Africa, in ships which trade for slaves, never return from thence. I dare not depend too much upon my memory, as to the number of ships and men employed in the slave trade more than thirty years ago; nor do I know what has been the state of the trade since; therefore I shall not attempt to make calculations. But, as I cannot but form some opinion upon the subject, I judge it probable, that the collective sum of seamen, who go from all our ports to Africa within the course of a year (taking Guinea into the extensive sense, from Goree or Gambia, and including the coast of Angola), cannot be less than eight thousand; and if, upon an average of ships and seasons, a fifth part of these die, the annual loss is fifteen hundred. I believe those who have taken pains to make more exact inquiries, will deem my supposition to be very moderate.

Thus much concerning the first evil, the loss of seamen and subjects, which the nation sustains by the African slave trade.

2. There is a second, which either is, or ought to be, deemed of importance, considered in a political light: I mean, the dreadful effects of this trade upon the minds of those who are engaged in it. There are,

doubtless, exceptions; and I would willingly except myself. But in general, I know of no method of getting money, not even that of robbing for it upon the highway, which has so direct a tendency to effacc the moral sense, to rob the heart of every gentle and humane disposition, and to harden it, like steel, against all impressions of sensibility.

Usually, about two-thirds of a cargo of slaves are males. When a hundred and fifty or two hundred stout men, torn from their native land, many of whom never saw the sea, much less a ship, till a short space before they had embarked; who have, probably, the same natural prejudice against a white man, as we have against a black; and who often bring with them an apprehension they are bought to be eaten: I say, when thus circumstanced, it is not to be expected that they will tamely resign themselves to their situation. It is always taken for granted, that they will attempt to gain their liberty if possible. Accordingly, as we dare not trust them, we receive them on board, from the first as enemies; and, before their number exceeds, perhaps, ten or fifteen, they are all put in irons; in most ships, two and two together. And frequently, they are not thus confined, as they might most conveniently stand or move, the right hand and foot of one to the left of the other, but across; that is, the hand and foot of each on the same side, whether right or left, are fettered together: so that they cannot move either hand or foot, but with great caution, and with perfect consent. Thus they must sit, walk, and lie, for many months (sometimes for nine or ten), without any mitigation or relief, unless they are sick.

In the night, they are confined below; in the daytime (if the weather be fine) they are upon deck; and as they are brought by pairs, a chain is put through a ring upon their irons, and this likewise locked down to the ringbolts, which are fastened, at certain intervals, upon the deck. These, and other precautions, are no more than necessary; especially, as while the number of slaves increases, that of the people who are to guard them, is diminished, by sickness, or death, or by being absent in the boats: so that, sometimes, not ten men can be mustered, to watch, night and day, over two hundred, besides having all the other business of the ship to attend.

That these precautions are so often effectual, is much more to be wondered at, than that they sometimes fail. One unguarded hour, or minute, is sufficient to give the slaves the opportunity they are always waiting for. An attempt to rise upon the ship's company, brings on instantaneous and horrid war: for, when they are once in motion, they are desperate; and where they do not conquer, they are seldom quelled without much mischief and bloodshed on both sides.

Sometimes, when the slaves are ripe for an insurrection, one of them will impeach the affair; and then necessity, and the state policy, of these small but most absolute governments, enforce maxims directly contrary to the nature of things. The traitor to the cause of liberty is caressed, rewarded, and deemed an honest fellow. The patriots, who formed and animated the plan, if they can be found out, must be treated as villains, and punished, to intimidate the rest. These punishments, in their nature and degree, depend upon the sovereign will of the captain. Some are content with inflicting such moderate punishment as may suffice for an example. But unlimited power, instigated by revenge, and where the heart, by a long familiarity with the sufferings of slaves, is become callous, and insensible to the pleadings of humanity, is terrible!

I have seen them sentenced to unmerciful whippings, continued till the poor creatures have not had power to groan under their misery, and hardly a sign of life has remained. I have seen them agonizing for hours, I believe for days together, under the torture of the thumbscrews; a dreadful engine, which, if the screw be turned by an unrelenting hand, can give intolerable anguish. There have been instances in which cruelty has proceeded still further; but, as I hope they are few, and I can mention but one from my own knowledge, I shall but mention it.

I have often heard a captain, who has been long since been dead, boast of his conduct in a former voyage, when his slaves attempted to rise upon him. After he had suppressed the insurrection, he sat in judgment upon the insurgents; and not only, in cold blood, adjudged several of them, I know not how many, to die, but studied, with no small attention, how to make death as excruciating as possible. For my reader's sake, I suppress the recital of particulars.

Surely, it must be allowed, that they who are long conversant with such scenes as these, are liable to imbibe a spirit of ferociousness, and savage insensibility, of which human nature, depraved as it is, is not, ordinarily, capable. If these things be true, the reader will admit the possibility of a fact that was in current report when I was upon the coast, and the truth of which, though I cannot now authenticate it, I have no reason to doubt.

A mate of a ship in a long-boat, purchased a young woman, with a fine child, of about a year old, in her arms. In the night, the child cried much, and disturbed his sleep. He rose up in great anger, and swore, that if the child did not cease making such a noise, he would presently silence it. The child continued to cry. At length he rose up a second time, tore the child from the mother, and threw it into the sea. The child was soon silenced indeed, but it was not so easy to pacify the woman: she was too valuable to be thrown overboard, and he was obliged to bear the sound of her lamentations, till he could put her on board his ship.

I am persuaded that every tender mother, who feasts her eyes and her mind when she contemplates the infant in her arms, will commiserate the poor Africans. But why do I speak of one child, when we have heard and read a melancholy story, too notoriously true to admit of contradiction, of more than a hundred grown slaves, thrown into the sea, at one time, from on board a ship, when fresh water was scarce; to fix the loss upon the underwriters, which otherwise, had they died on board, must have fallen upon the owners of the vessel. These instances are specimens of the spirit produced, by the African trade, in men, who, once, were no more destitute of the milk of human kindness than ourselves.

Hitherto, I have considered the condition of the men slaves only. From the women, there is no danger of insurrection, and they are carefully kept from the men; I mean from the black men. But in what I have to offer, on this head, I am far from including every ship. I speak not of what is universally, but of what is too commonly, and I am afraid, too generally, prevalent.

I have already observed, that the captain of an African ship, while upon the coast, is absolute in his command; and if he be humane, vigilant, and determined, he has it in his power to protect the miserable; for scarcely any thing can be done on board the ship, without his permission or connivance. But this power is too seldom exerted in favour of the poor women slaves.

When we hear of a town taken by storm, and given up to the ravages of an enraged and licentious army, of wild and unprincipled Cossacks, perhaps no part of the distress affects a feeling mind more, than the treatment to which the women are exposed. But the enormities frequently committed in an African ship, though equally flagrant, are little known *here,* and are considered *there,* only as matters of course. When the women and girls are taken on board a ship, naked, trembling, terrified, perhaps almost exhausted with cold, fatigue, and hunger, they are often exposed to the wanton rudeness of white savages. The poor creatures cannot understand the language they hear, but the looks and manner of the speakers are sufficiently intelligible. In imagination, the prey is divided, upon the spot, and only reserved till opportunity offers. Where resistance or refusal, would be utterly in vain, even the solicitation of consent is seldom thought of. But I forbear.—This is not a subject for declamation. Facts like these, so certain and so numerous, speak for themselves. Surely, if the advocates for the Slave Trade attempt to plead for it, before the wives and daughters of our happy land, or before those who have wives or daughters of their own, they must lose their cause.

Perhaps some hard-hearted pleader may suggest, that such treatment would indeed be cruel, in Europe: but the African women are negroes, savages, who have no idea of the nicer sensations which obtain among civilized people. I dare contradict them in the strongest terms. I have lived long, and conversed much, amongst these supposed savages. I have often slept in their towns, in a house filled with goods for trade, with no person in the house but myself, and with no other door than a mat; in that security, which no man in his senses would expect in this civilized nation, especially in this metropolis, without the precaution of having strong doors, strongly locked and bolted. And with regard to the women, in

Sherbro, where I was most acquainted, I have seen many instances of modesty, and even delicacy, which would not disgrace an English woman. Yet, such is the treatment which I have known permitted, if not encouraged, in many of our ships—they have been abandoned, without restraint, to the lawless will of the first comer.

Accustomed thus to despise, insult, and injure the slaves on board, it may be expected that the conduct of many of our people to the natives, with whom they trade, is, as far as circumstances admit, very similar; and it is so. They are considered as a people to be robbed and spoiled with impunity. Every art is employed to deceive and wrong them. And he who has most address in this way, has most to boast of.

Not an article that is capable of diminution or adulteration, is delivered genuine, or entire. The spirits are lowered by water. False heads are put into the kegs that contain the gunpowder; so that, though the keg appears large, there is no more powder in it, than in a much smaller. The linen and cotton cloths are opened, and two or three yards, according to the length of the piece, cut off, not from the end, but out of the middle, where it is not so readily noticed.

The natives are cheated, in the number, weight, measure, or quality of what they purchase, in every possible way: and, by habit and emulation, a marvellous dexterity is acquired in these practices. And thus the natives in their turn, in proportion to their commerce with the Europeans, and (I am sorry to add) particularly with the English, become jealous, insidious, and revengeful.

They know with whom they deal, and are accordingly prepared;—though they can trust some ships and boats, which have treated them with punctuality, and may be trusted by them. A quarrel, sometimes, furnishes pretext for detaining, and carrying away, one or more of the natives, which is retaliated, if practicable, upon the next boat that comes to the place, from the same port. For so far their vindictive temper is restrained by their ideas of justice, that they will not, often, revenge an injury received from a Liverpool ship, upon one belonging to Bristol or London.

They will usually wait with patience the arrival of one, which, they suppose, by her sailing from the same place, has some connection with that which used them ill; and they are so quick at distinguishing our little local differences of language and customs in a ship, that before they have been in a ship five minutes, and often before they come on board, they know, with certainty, whether she be from Bristol, Liverpool, or London.

Retaliation on their parts, furnishes a plea for reprisal on ours. Thus, in one place or another, trade is often suspended, all intercourse cut off, and things are in a state of war; till necessity, either on the ship's part or on theirs, produces overtures of peace, and dictates the price, which the offending party must pay for it. But it is a warlike peace. We trade under arms; and they are furnished with long knives.

For, with a few exceptions, the English and the Africans, reciprocally, consider each other as consummate villains, who are always watching opportunities to do mischief. In short, we have, I fear too deservedly, a very unfavourable character upon the coast. When I have charged a black with unfairness and dishonesty, he has answered, if able to clear himself, with an air of disdain, 'What! do you think I am a white man?'

Such is the nature, such are the concomitants, of the slave trade; and such is the school in which many thousands of our seamen are brought up. Can we, then wonder at that impatience of subordination, and that disposition to mutiny, amongst them, which has been of late, so loudly complained of, and so severely felt? Will not sound policy suggest the necessity of some expedient here? Or can sound policy suggest any effectual expedient, but the total suppression of a trade, which, like a poisonous root, diffuses its malignity into every branch?

The effects which our trade has upon the blacks, those especially who come under our power, may be considered under three heads,—How they are acquired? The mortality they are subject to! and, How those who survive are disposed of?

I confine my remarks on the first head to the Windward coast, and can speak most confidently of the trade in Sherbro, where I lived. I own, however, that I question, if any part of the Windward coast is equal to Sherbro, in point of regularity and government. They have no men of great power or property among them; as I am told there are upon the Gold coast, at Whida and Benin. The Sherbro people live much in the patriarchal way. An old man usually presides in each town, whose authority depends more on his years, than on his possessions: and he, who is called the king, is not easily distinguished, either by state or wealth, from the rest. But the different districts, which seem to be, in many respects, independent of each other, are incorporated, and united, by means of an institution which pervades them all, and is called the Purrow. The persons of this order, who are very numerous, seem, very much, to resemble the Druids, who once presided in our island.

The Purrow has both the legislative and executive authority, and, under their sanction, there is a police exercised, which is by no means contemptible. Every thing belonging to the Purrow is mysterious and severe, but, upon the whole, it has very good effects; and as any man, whether bond or free, who will submit to be initiated into their mysteries, may be admitted of the order, it is a kind of commonwealth. And, perhaps, few people enjoy more, simple, political freedom, than the inhabitants of Sherbro, belonging to the Purrow (who are not slaves), further than they are bound by their own institutions. Private property is tolerably well secured, and violence is much suppressed.

The state of slavery, among these wild barbarous people, as we esteem them, is much milder than in our colonies. For as, on the one hand, they have no land in high cultivation, like our West India plantations, and therefore no call for that execessive, unintermitted labour, which exhausts our slaves; so, on the other hand, no man is permitted to draw blood even from a slave. If he does, he is liable to a strict inquisition; for the Purrow laws will not allow a private individual to shed blood. A man may sell his slave, if he pleases; but he may not wantonly abuse him. The laws, likewise, punish some species of theft with slavery; and in cases of adultery, which are very common, as polygamy is the custom of the country, both the woman, and the man who offends with her, are liable to be sold for slaves, unless they can satisfy the husband, or unless they are redeemed by their friends.

Among these unenlightened blacks, it is a general maxim, that if a man steals, or breaks a moveable, as a musket, for instance, the offence may be nearly compensated by putting another musket in its place; but offences, which cannot be repaired in kind, as adultery, admit of no satisfaction, till the injured person declares that he is satisfied. So that, if a rich man seduces the wife of a poor man, he has it in his power to change places with him; for he may send for every article in his house, one by one, till he says, 'I have enough'. The only alternative, is personal slavery.

I suppose, bribery and influence may have their effects in Guinea, as they have in some other countries; but their laws in the main are wise and good, and, upon the whole, they have considerable operation; and therefore, I believe many of the slaves purchased in Sherbro, and probably upon the whole Windward coast, are convicts, who have forfeited their liberty, by breaking the laws of their country.

But I apprehend, that the neighbourhood of our ships, and the desire of our goods, are motives which often push the rigour of the laws to an extreme, which would not be exacted, if they were left to themselves.

But slaves are the staple article of the traffic; and though a considerable number may have been born near the sea, I believe the bulk of them are brought from far. I have reason to think that some travel more than a thousand miles, before they reach the sea-coast. Whether there may be convicts amongst these likewise, or what proportion they may bear to those who are taken prisoners in war, it is impossible to know.

I judge, the principal source of the slave trade, is, the wars which prevail among the natives. Sometimes these wars break out between those who live near the sea. The English, and other Europeans, have been charged with fomenting them; I believe (so far as concerns the Windward coast) unjustly. That some would do it, if they could, I doubt not; but I do not think they can have opportunity. Nor is it needful they should interfere. Thousands, in our own country, wish for war, because they fatten upon its spoils.

Human nature is much the same in every place, and few people will be willing to allow, that the negroes in Africa are better than themselves.

Supposing, therefore, they wish for European goods, may not they wish to purchase them from a ship just arrived? Of course, they must wish for slaves to go to market with; and if they have not slaves, and think themselves strong enough to invade their neighbours, they will probably wish for war.—And if once they wish for it, how easy it is to find, or to make, pretexts for breaking an inconvenient peace; or (after the example of greater heroes, of Christian name) to make depredations, without condescending to assign any reasons.

I verily believe, that the far greater part of the wars, in Africa, would cease, if the Europeans would cease to tempt them, by offering goods for slaves. And though they do not bring legions into the field, their wars are bloody. I believe, the captives reserved for sale are fewer than the slain.

I have not sufficient data to warrant calculation, but, I suppose, not less than one hundred thousand slaves are exported, annually, from all parts of Africa, and that more than one-half of these are exported in English bottoms.

If but an equal number are killed in war, and if many of these wars are kindled by the incentive of selling their prisoners; what an annual accumulation of blood must there be, crying against the nations of Europe concerned in this trade, and particularly against our own!

I have often been gravely told, as a proof that the Africans, however hardly treated, deserve but little compassion, that they are a people so destitute of natural affection, that it is common among them for parents to sell their children, and children their parents. And, I think, a charge of this kind is brought against them by the respectable author of *Spectacle de la Nature*. But he must have been misinformed. I never heard of one instance of either, while I used the Coast.

One article more upon this head, is kidnapping, or stealing free people. Some people suppose, that the ship trade is rather the stealing, than the buying of slaves. But there is enough to lay to the charge of the ships, without accusing them falsely. The slaves, in general, are bought, and paid for. Sometimes, when goods are lent, or trusted on shore, the trader voluntarily leaves a free person, perhaps his own son, as a hostage, or pawn, for the payment; and, in case of default, the hostage is carried off, and sold; which, however hard upon him, being in consequence of a free stipulation, cannot be deemed unfair. There have been instances of unprincipled captains, who, at the close of what they supposed their last voyage, and when they had no intention of revisiting the coast, have detained, and carried away, free people with them; and left the next ship, that should come from the same port to risk the consequences. But these actions, I hope and believe, are not common.

With regard to the natives, to steal a free man or woman, and to sell them on board a ship, would, I think, be a more difficult and more dangerous attempt in Sherbro, than in London. But I have no doubt, that the traders who come, from the interior parts of Africa, at a great distance, find opportunity, in the course of their journey, to pick up stragglers, whom they may meet in their way. This branch of oppression and robbery would likewise fail, if the temptation to it were removed.

I have, to the best of my knowledge, pointed out the principal sources of that immense supply of slaves which furnishes so large an exportation every year. If all that are taken on board the ships were to survive the voyage, and be landed in good order, possibly the English, French, and Dutch islands and colonies would be soon overstocked, and fewer ships would sail to the coast. But a large abatement must be made for mortality.—After what I have already said of their treatment, I shall now, that I am again to consider them on board the ships, confine myself to this point.

In the Portuguese ships, which trade from Brazil to the Gold coast and Angola, I believe, a heavy mortality is not frequent. The slaves have room, they are not put in irons (I speak from information only), and are humanely treated.

With our ships, the great object is, to be full. When the ship is there, it is thought desirable she should take as many as possible. The cargo of a vessel of a hundred tons, or little more, is calculated to purchase from two hundred and twenty to two hundred and fifty slaves. Their lodging-rooms below the deck, which are three (for the men, the boys, and the women), besides a place for the sick, are sometimes more than five feet high, and sometimes less; and this height is divided towards the middle, for the slaves lie in two rows, one above the other, on each side of the ship, close to each other, like books upon a shelf. I have known them so close, that the shelf would not, easily, contain one more. And I have known a white man sent down, among the men, to lay them in these rows to the greatest advantage, so that as little space as possible might be lost.

Let it be observed, that the poor creatures, thus cramped for want of room, are likewise in irons, for the most part both hands and feet, and two together, which makes it difficult for them to turn or move, to attempt either to rise or to lie down, without hurting themselves, or each other. Nor is the motion of the ship, especially her heeling, or stoop on one side, when under sail, to be omitted; for this, as they lie athwart, or cross the ship, adds to the uncomfortableness of their lodging, especially to those who lie on the leeward or leaning side of the vessel.

Dire is the tossing, deep the groans.—

The heat and smell of these rooms, when the weather will not admit of the slaves being brought upon deck, and of having their rooms cleaned every day, would be almost insupportable to a person not accustomed to them. If the slaves and their rooms can be constantly aired, and they are not detained too long on board, perhaps there are not many die; but the contrary is often their lot. They are kept down, by the weather, to breathe a hot and corrupted air, sometimes for a week: this, added to the galling of their irons, and the despondency which seizes their spirits when thus confined, soon becomes fatal. And every morning, perhaps, more instances than one are found, of the living and the dead, like the captives of Mezentius, fastened together.

Epidemical fevers and fluxes, which fill the ship with noisome and noxious effluvia, often break out, and infect the seamen likewise, and thus the oppressors, and the oppressed, fall by the same stroke. I believe, nearly one-half of the slaves on board, have, sometimes, died; and that the loss of a third part, in these circumstances, is not unusual. The ship, in which I was mate, left the coast with two hundred and eighteen slaves on board; and though we were not much affected by epidemical disorders, I find by my journal of that voyage (now before me), that we buried sixty-two on our passage to South Carolina, exclusive of those which died before we left the coast, of which I have no account.

I believe, upon an average between the more healthy, and the more sickly voyages, and including all contingencies, one fourth of the whole purchase may be allotted to the article of mortality: that is, if the English ships purchase *sixty thousand slaves* annually, upon the whole extent of the coast, the annual loss of lives cannot be much less than *fifteen thousand*.

I am now to speak of the survivors.—When the ships make the land (usually the West India islands), and have their port in view, after having been four, five, six weeks, or a longer time, at sea (which depends much upon the time that passes before they can get into the permanent trade-winds, which blow from the north-east and east across the Atlantic), then, and not before, they venture to release the men slaves from their irons: and then, the sight of the land, and their freedom from long and painful confinement, usually excite in them a degree of alacrity, and a transient feeling of joy—

The prisoner leaps to lose his chains.

But this joy is short-lived indeed. The condition of the unhappy slaves is in a continual progress from bad to worse. Their case is truly pitiable, from the moment they are in a state of slavery in their own country; but it may be deemed a state of ease and liberty, compared with their situation on board our ships.

Yet, perhaps, they would wish to spend the remainder of their days on ship-board, could they know, beforehand, the nature of the servitude which awaits them on shore; and that the dreadful hardships and sufferings they have already endured, would, to the most of them, only terminate in excessive toil, hunger, and the excruciating tortures of the cart-whip, inflicted at the caprice of an unfeeling overseer, proud of the power allowed him of punishing whom, and when, and how he pleases.

I hope the slaves, in our islands, are better treated now, than they were at the time when I was in the trade. And, even then, I know there were slaves, who, under the care and protection of humane masters, were, comparatively, happy. But I saw and heard enough to satisfy me, that their condition, in general, was wretched to the extreme. However, my stay in Antigua and St Christopher's (the only islands I visited) was too short, to qualify me for saying much, from my own certain knowledge, upon this painful subject. Nor is it needful: —enough has been offered by several respectable writers, who have had opportunity of collecting surer and fuller information.

One thing I cannot omit, which was told me by the gentleman to whom my ship was consigned, at Antigua, in the year 1751, and who was himself a planter. He said, that calculations had been made, with all possible exactness, to determine which was the preferable, that is, the more saving method of managing slaves:

> 'Whether, to appoint them moderate work, plenty of provision, and such treatment as might enable them to protract their lives to old age?' Or,
>
> 'By rigorously straining their strength to the utmost, with little relaxation, hard fare, and hard usage, to wear them out before they became useless, and unable to do service; and then, to buy new ones, to fill up their places?'

He farther said, that these skilful calculators had determined in favour of the latter mode, as much the cheaper; and that he could mention several estates, in the island of Antigua, on which it was seldom known that a slave had lived above nine years.—*Ex pede Herculem*! [1]

When the slaves are landed for sale (for in the Leeward Islands they are usually sold on shore), it may happen, that after a long separation in different parts of the ship, when they are brought together in one place, some who are nearly related may recognize each other. If, upon such a meeting, pleasure should be felt, it can be but momentary. The sale disperses them wide, to different parts of the island, or to different islands. Husbands and wives, parents and children, brothers and sisters, must suddenly part again, probably to meet no more.

After a careful perusal of what I have written, weighing every paragraph distinctly, I can find nothing to retract. As it is not easy to write altogether with coolness upon this business, and especially not easy to me, who have formerly been so deeply engaged in it; I have been jealous, lest the warmth of imagination might have insensibly seduced me, to aggravate and over-

[[1] Hercules from his foot – judge the whole from a part.]

charge some of the horrid features, which I have attempted to delineate, of the African trade. But, upon a strict review, I am satisfied.

I have apprised the reader, that I write from memory, after an interval of more than thirty years. But at the same time, I believe, many things which I saw, heard, and felt, upon the coast of Africa, are so deeply engraven in my memory, that I can hardly forget, or greatly mistake them, while I am capable of remembering any thing. I am certainly not guilty of wilful misrepresentation. And, upon the whole, I dare appeal to the Great Searcher of hearts, in whose presence I write, and before whom I, and my readers, must all shortly appear, that (with the restrictions and exceptions I have made) I have advanced nothing, but what, to the best of my judgement and conscience, is true.

I have likewise written without solicitation, and simply from the motive I have already assigned; a conviction, that the share I have formerly had in the trade, binds me, in conscience, to throw what light I am able upon the subject, now it is likely to become a point of parliamentary investigation.

No one can have less interest in it that I have at present, further than as I am interested by the feelings of humanity, and a regard for the honour and welfare of my country.

Though unwilling to give offence to a single person, in such a cause, I ought not to be afraid of offending many, by declaring the truth. If, indeed, there can be many, whom even interest can prevail upon to contradict the common sense of mankind, by pleading for a commerce so iniquitous, so cruel, so oppressive, so destructive, as the African Slave Trade!

Finis

Glossary

Definitions of nautical terms are based on *Burney's Maritime Dictionary* and weights and measures on *Dr Johnson's Dictionary*.

AMPLITUDE: the magnetical amplitude is the arc of the horizon contained between the sun at the time of its setting and magnetic west; the difference between this and the true amplitude is the variation of the compass.

ANCHOR (of brandy): an obsolete form of *anker*; 10 old wine gallons or 8⅓ imperial gallons.

ANCHORS:

BOWER (B.B. or BEST BOWER): the main anchor, hung in the bows next in size to the sheet anchor.

KEDGE: the smallest anchor.

SHEET: the largest anchor, only used in emergencies.

APEAK: vertically, an anchor is a-peak when the cable has been drawn so tight as to bring the ship directly over it.

BAR: a unit of currency, see page xv.

BARRATRY: in marine law, fraud or gross and criminal negligence to the prejudice of the owners.

BAFTS, BASTS: a cheap woven cloth.

B.B., BEST BOWER: *see* ANCHOR.

BEND: to tie, to make fast.

BENDS, BENTS: the main planks on the ship's side.

BOOBY: a species of gannet so called because it can be caught by hand.

BOWER: *see* ANCHOR.

BRIG: a vessel similar to a snow (*see* page 117), but carrying the trysail on the mainmast.

BUTT: a vessel for wine, beer, or dry food (e.g. currants) from 15 to 22 hundredweight.

CAG, KEG: a barrel, capacity 4 or 5 gallons.

CALK: to stop up the seams of a ship.

CAMWOOD: African *Kambi*, a red wood used for dye, furniture, and violin bows.

CHANNEL BEND: thick planks projecting from the ship's side to extend the shrouds.

CLEAR HAUSE: to untangle the anchor cables.

CLEW: the lower corner of a square sail, or the after lower corner of a fore-and-aft sail.

CLINCH: to fasten a cable with a half hitch, and then lash the end back on to the cable.

DOGGER: a fishing-vessel similar to a ketch.

FLUX: an abnormal copious flowing of blood, excrements, etc., from the bowels or other organs. An early name for dysentery.

FRAP: to tighten lashings by drawing and tying them together with another rope.

FRET, FRETT: a gust or squall of wind.

F.T.G.: *see* page 117.

GAFF: a spart to extend the head of the trysail.

GANG CASK: a water cask.

GRAPLIN, GRAPLING, GRAPNEL: a small sort of anchor fitted with hooks or claws.

GRATINGS: open-work or latticed coverings for the hatches.

GRIMETAR: probably the same as *gromettos* or *gremetoes*, 'black saylors, commonly known by the name of gremetoes, free people who volunterely went with us . . . for a small demand of wages . . .' (Nics Owen).

GRIPE: a lashing to secure a boat on the deck.

HAND: a bundle of tobacco leaves tied together.

HAND: to furl.

HAUL: to sail the ship nearer to the wind than before; a ship close hauled is sailing as near to the wind as possible.

JIB BOOM: a movable spar running out beyond the bowsprit.

KEDGE: *see* ANCHORS.

KEG: *see* CAG.

KETCH: a small two-masted vessel with square and fore-and-aft sails.

LEAGUE: 3 nautical miles or nearly 3½ statute miles.

LONGBOAT: the largest boat carried by a ship, often rigged as a small sloop.

LUGSAIL: a four-cornered sail set on a yard that hangs obliquely to the mast.

M.T.G.: *see* page 117.

M.T.S.: *see* page 117.

MAIN CHAINS: iron plates on the ship's side, through which the main shrouds are fastened.

NICANNERS: a textile formerly imported from India. More usual spellings were *Niccanees* or *Nicanees*, and Clarkson mentions them in connection with the slave trade as *Nicamees*.

PIPE: a wooden barrel, capacity 2 hogsheads, 126 gallons.

PLANTANE: a species of banana.

PLYER: a ship beating up against the wind.

PUNCHEON: a large cask for liquids.

QUINTAL: a hundredweight to weigh with, hence, probably 100 lbs.

REAVE, REEF, REAF: part of the sail gathered up so as to shorten sail.

REEVE: to thread a rope through a pulley or hole.

SAILS: *see* page 117, and also under LUGSAIL, STAYSAIL, and STEERING SAIL.

SCHOONER: a two- or three-masted vessel with fore-and-aft rigging.

SERVILAS, SCREVELOS: small elephant tusks.

SHALOP, SHALLOP: a boat fitted with sails, similar to a longboat but of a shallower draught.

SHEET: *see* ANCHORS.

SHEATHING: a protective covering to the bottom of a ship.

SHIP: a term particularly applied to three-masted square-rigged vessels.

SHROUDS: large ropes extending from the mast to the sides of the ship to support the mast.

SINNETT: a braided cordage.

SLOOP: a single-masted vessel with fore-and-aft rigging.

SNOW: *see* page 117.

SPOON-DRIFT: spray from the tops of waves driven continuously along the surface of the sea, now known as spindrift.

STAND: the difference between standing and stretching is in the amount of sail a ship carries. The ship stands under easy sail, and stretches under a crowd of sail.

STANTIENTS: stanchions, posts used as vertical supports.

START: to empty when applied to liquids, but to any weight such as the anchor it means to move.

STAY: a rope holding a mast or spar.

BACK STAY: a rope running from the topmast head to the side of the ship.

STAYSAIL: a sail set on a fore-and-aft stay between the masts.

STEERING SAIL: another name for studding sails, sails set on small extra yards outside the square sails and used in light winds.

STIFF: upright, having the ability to carry sail without capsizing.

STOPPER: a short rope for making something fast.

STRETCH: *see* STAND.

SWIVEL: a cannon mounted on a swivel on the gunwale, or shot for such cannon.

TEER, TIER: a large rack in which anchors, cables, tackles, butts, etc., are stored.

TEMONEERS, TIMONEERS: helmsmen.

TIERCE: a vessel holding the third part of a pipe or 35 gallons.

TOOTH: an elephant's tusk.

TRIP: to loose the anchor from its bed and to raise it just clear of the bottom with the cable or the buoy rope.

VEER: of cables—to let out or slacken, or change.

WASHBOARDS: boards attached to the gunwale to stop water washing in.

WORE: past tense of *wear*, to put a ship about bringing her stern to windward.

YAUL, YAWL: a small boat with six oars and sails for carrying light stores or passengers to and from a ship.

A SNOW

Redrawn from *Rigging and Seamanship*, Vol I (1794)

1. Bowsprit
2. Foremast
3. Mainmast
4. Spritsail
5. Jib
6. Fore topgallant sail (F.T.G.)
7. Fore topsail
8. Foresail
9. Main topgallant sail (M.T.G.)
10. Main topsail (M.T.S.)
11. Mainsail
12. Trysail

See also under GAFF, JIB BOOM, STAYSAIL, STEERING SAIL, etc.

INDEX